Telephone Communication
in the Information Age

Roberta Mantus
President, Mantus Creative Consultants

Roberta Moore
Educational Publishing Consultant

South-Western Educational Publishing

Editor-in-Chief: Robert E. First
Developmental Editor: Inell Bolls
Marketing Manager: Al Roane
Production Coordinator: Jane Congdon
Production Editor: Denise A. Wheeler
Production Services: Kristina Almquist Design

ISBN: 0-538-71514-6

2 3 4 5 8 7 PR 01

Printed in the United States of America

I(T)P
International Thomson Publishing

South-Western Educational Publishing is a division of International Thomson Publishing, Inc. The ITP trademark is used under license.

Library of Congress Cataloging-in-Publication Data

Mantus, Roberta.
    Telephone communication in the information age / Roberta Mantus and Roberta Moore.
        p.   cm.
    Includes index.
    ISBN 0-538-71514-6
    1. Telephone in business. 2. Telephone etiquette. I. Moore, Roberta, 1947-   . II. Title.
HF5541.T4M36 1996
651.7'3—dc20   95-37276
                                                          CIP

PREFACE

In the light of human history, the invention of the telephone happened just the blink of an eye ago. Since the time that Alexander Graham Bell invented the first working telephone in 1876, the concept of communicating electronically across distances has taken giant leaps forward. Today telephone and telecommunications technology enable us to reach all parts of the world in an instant—and not only with our voices. Images can be transmitted via telephone lines in the form of facsimile communications and videophones. Cellular communications and satellite transmission enable us to be anywhere and reach anyone by phone. Progress continues to be made in telecommunications to the extent that it is almost impossible to keep current with the advances.

The telephone and related technologies are among the most vital kinds of office equipment. However, without employees who are skilled in using the equipment, the technology has little importance of its own. Workers in offices today must apply two kinds of skills to effectively harness the power of the technology. They must understand the equipment and technology, and they must have strong personal communications skills.

Managers have placed great emphasis on communications skills as American business has evolved in recent years. In the last decade, a troubled national economy and strong foreign competition forced managers of U.S. companies to examine their position in the marketplace and determine what they could do to improve business and regain the confidence and trust of American consumers. One answer to the problem was to focus on quality—of goods and services. Customer service has proved to be a key element in providing businesses with a competitive edge. Any employee who answers a telephone is actively involved in customer service and participates in enhancing the image and reputation of a company. Hence, workers today must combine personal and technical communications skills in order to function appropriately and effectively.

TEXT CONTENT AND ORGANIZATION

Telephone Communication in the Information Age has a dual focus on technology and personal communications skills. Chapter 1 introduces the reader to both subjects within the context of the quality approach to communication. Chapter 2 covers telephone and telecommunications systems, equipment, and technology. In subsequent chapters, the technology is integrated with discussions and applications of communications skills.

Chapter 3 provides the foundation for communications skills by covering speaking and listening skills. Chapter 4 focuses on making and receiving calls. Chapter 5 covers telephone management and provides information for support and professional employees on making arrangements and placing orders over the phone. A section is also included on conducting research. Chapter 6 presents international communications by covering procedures for using the technology and information on intercultural communications.

Chapter 7 provides a view of telemarketing—different kinds of telemarketing and telemarketing jobs. Chapter 8 offers general information and guidelines for working with customers and the public. It also offers a view of customer service departments—job qualifications, training, and organization. The three appendixes provide reference information on national and international area codes and the 24-hour clock.

CHAPTER FEATURES

Each chapter has special features designed to enhance the knowledge and skills of the readers with respect to technology and communications skills.

- **On the Job** is a feature that begins each chapter. In each case, a real-world job situation is presented in which a worker uses the telephone in a way that illustrates the content of the chapter. Written dialogue is often included.
- **411** is a feature that provides special information on telephone and telecommunications technology or on the telecommunications industry.
- **Written dialogues** provide real-world situations that students must analyze and evaluate.
- **Audio dialogues** are provided on a cassette. These dialogues also contain real-world situations that address the issues discussed in the text. Students listen, analyze the dialogues, and apply problem-solving skills.

An instructor's manual, containing suggestions for teaching the course, keys, and examination questions, is also available.

All the elements of *Telephone Communication in the Information Age* combine to make the text essential for preparing students to work in the office of today.

Roberta Mantus
Roberta Moore

ABOUT THE
AUTHORS

Roberta Mantus is president of Mantus Creative Consultants, a company that creates and develops educational materials for a variety of publishing companies. Her experience in educational publishing spans more than 20 years. Before starting her own company, she served as executive editor, where she was responsible for publishing multimedia materials (books, audio- and videotapes, and computer software) in several subject areas including information processing, information management, desktop publishing, computer technology, and secretarial studies. Other texts written by Ms. Mantus include *Design Guidelines for Desktop Publishing* and *Everyday Forms*.

Roberta Moore is an educational publishing consultant and writer who has worked in educational publishing since 1976. In the course of a 15-year career as editor, editor-in-chief, and editorial director, she participated in the creation and development of hundreds of educational and training materials. The books, videos, and software products she has developed cover a range of fields, including career development, communications, secretarial training, adult basic education, and computer technology. She is now president of her own company, Roberta Moore Publishing Services, offering writing, project management, and management consulting services to major publishing companies throughout the United States.

ACKNOWLEDGMENTS

The authors are grateful to the following reviewers for their insight and helpful suggestions:

Carol L. Libson, Hennepin Technical College, Minneapolis, Minnesota

Anita P. Gibson, Training Inc., Indianapolis, Indiana

Pat Liford, Customer Service Manager, Delmar Publishers, Albany, New York

Olive D. Church, University of Wyoming, Laramie, Wyoming

Lydia M. Gordon, New York City Technical College, New York, NY

Candie L. Hurley, District Manager, Video Technical Center, AT&T, Englewood, Colorado.

CONTENTS

CHAPTER 1   Telecommunications in Business   1

On the Job **1**; Objectives **2**; Telecommunications Technology **2**;
The Communications Process **4**; The Telephone as a Communications
Tool **4**; Communications Skills **7**; The Quality Approach to
Communication **7**; Basic Communication and Problem-Solving Skills **8**;
Your Telephone Persona **9**; Chapter Summary **11**; Key Terms **11**;
Chapter Review **12**

CHAPTER 2   Communications Systems and Equipment   17

On the Job **17**; Objectives **18**; Communications Systems **18**;
Centralized Systems **18**; Decentralized Systems **19**; Telephone
Equipment **22**; Standard Equipment and Features **22**;
Speakerphones **23**; Videophones **23**; Mobile Telephone Equipment **25**;
Telecommunications Technology **26**; Facsimile Transmission **26**;
Voice Processing **28**; Teleconferencing **29**; Telephone Service
Providers **30**; Chapter Summary **31**; Key Terms **32**; Chapter Review **33**

CHAPTER 3   Basic Telephone Communications Skills   37

On the Job **37**; Objectives **38**; Effective Communication **39**;
How Communication Works **39**; The Importance of Feedback **40**;
Avoid Distractions **41**; Speaking Skills **42**; Pace **42**; Modulation **42**;
Tone **43**; Pronunciation **43**; Enunciation **43**; Grammar **43**;
Vocabulary **44**; Local Regional Expressions **44**; National
Expressions **45**; Accents **46**; Audible and Verbal Distractions **47**;
Attitude **47**; Listening Skills **48**; Focus Your Attention **48**; Provide
Feedback **48**; Handle Difficulties **48**; Chapter Summary **49**; Key
Terms **49**; Chapter Review **50**

CHAPTER 4 Receiving and Making Calls   53

On the Job **53**; Objectives **54**; Receiving Calls **55**;
Answering the Phone **55**; Using Voice Mail **56**; Arranging
Phone Coverage **56**; Taking Messages **57**; Putting Callers on
Hold and Transferring Calls **57**; Being Put on the Spot **58**;
Dealing with Unwanted Callers **59**; Handling Problem Calls **60**;
Making Calls **60**; Types of Calls **60**; Sending Faxes **64**; Planning
Calls **65**; Leaving Messages **66**; Maintaining Confidentiality **67**;
Chapter Summary **67**; Key Terms **68**; Chapter Review **69**

CHAPTER 5 Professional Telephone Management   73

On the Job **73**; Objectives **74**; Handling Administrative
Procedures **74**; Answering for the Manager **74**; Keeping Telephone
Records **76**; Conducting Telephone Research **77**; Using Telephone
Directories **77**; Locating People **78**; Locating Information **79**;
Making Arrangements over the Phone **80**; Scheduling Meetings and
Appointments **80**; Making Reservations **82**; Placing Orders **84**;
Handling Teleconferences **84**; Arranging the Call **85**; During the
Call **85**; Chapter Summary **86**; Key Terms **86**; Chapter Review **87**

CHAPTER 6 International Telephone Communications   91

On the Job **91**; Objectives **92**; International Calling Procedures **92**;
Locating Information **93**; Placing International Calls **93**; Using Trans-
lation Services **94**; Crossing Time Zones **94**; The 24-Hour Clock **96**;
Intercultural Communications **97**; International Business
Procedures **97**; Adjusting to Cultural Differences **99**; Overcoming
Language Barriers **100**; Learning about Other Cultures **101**;
Chapter Summary **102**; Key Terms **102**; Chapter Review **103**

CHAPTER 7 Telemarketing   107

On the Job **107**; Objectives **108**; The Telemarketing Concept **109**;
Types of Telemarketing **109**; Telemarketing Skills **110**; Uses of
Telemarketing **111**; Telemarketing Sales **111**; Key Aspects of
Selling **111**; The Seven-Step Selling Process **112**; Market
Research **116**; Point-of-Sale Market Research **116**; Telephone
Surveys **117**; Fund-Raising **120**; Fund-Raising Techniques **120**;
The Fund-Raising Process **120**; The Telemarketing Field **121**;
Chapter Summary **124**; Key Terms **125**; Chapter Review **126**

CHAPTER 8 Customer Service   131

On the Job **131**; Objectives **132**; General Procedures **133**; Learn about
Your Company **133**; Learn about Your Department **133**; Learn about
the Product or Service **133**; Learn about Your Equipment **134**;
Customer Service Departments **135**; Job Qualifications **135**;
Training **136**; Organization of Departments **139**; Dealing with
Stress **139**; Dealing with Customers **140**; Do's and Don'ts **140**;
Handling Problem Calls **142**; Chapter Summary **143**; Key Terms **143**;
Chapter Review **144**

APPENDIX A
Area Codes for Major Cities in the United States and Territories **147**

APPENDIX B
International Calling Codes for Countries and Major Cities **151**

APPENDIX C
The 24-Hour Clock **155**

INDEX **156**

TELECOMMUNICATIONS IN BUSINESS

On the Job: Technology Reduces Stress

Jeff Maglie works in the production department of an architectural design firm in Baltimore, Maryland. His company, Lowe and Heatherington Design Associates, is in the process of revising the plans for a major design job for Fulton's, a department store in Portland, Oregon. The plans must be shipped by the end of work today, and everyone has been working furiously to get them completed on time. At 12:30 p.m., Jeff's telephone rings.

Jeff: Lowe and Heatherington Production Department, Jeff Maglie speaking.

Gloria: Hi, Jeff, this is Gloria Emerson calling from Fulton's.

Jeff: Hello, Gloria, what can I do for you?

Gloria: I know the plans for the store renovations aren't due until tomorrow, but I have to prepare the budget spreadsheets today. I just found out that my boss has to present the revised plans and budgets to the board tomorrow afternoon. I was wondering if you could read me the revised cost figures for the changes you're making.

Jeff: I'd like to help you, but I don't think I have time to read you all those figures over the phone. I've got just enough hours left in the day to put the finishing touches on the plans in order to ship them to you by overnight mail.

Gloria: Oh dear, without those figures I don't know how I'll get this presentation ready on time.

Jeff: Don't worry, Gloria. Here's what I'll do. When my assistant comes back from lunch at one o'clock, I'll have her pull the list of revised figures out of the plan and fax a copy to you. You'll have it in about half an hour.

Gloria: Thanks, Jeff. That'll give me the rest of the day to work on that budget.

Jeff: You're welcome. And if you have any questions on the costs, just give me a call before 5:30 Eastern time.

Gloria: I'll do that. Good-bye, and thanks again.

Jeff: Good-bye.

In this scenario, Jeff was able to help Gloria without using up valuable time needed for his own work. At the same time, Gloria was able to complete her boss's presentation without jeopardizing the larger goal of getting the final proposal finished on schedule. Technology saved both people from having to engage in a a stressful rush to meet the deadline for an important project.

Objectives

After completing this chapter, you should be able to:

- Recognize the field of telecommunications as a key area of growth and change that is driving technology advances in the Information Age.

- Understand how telecommunications technology exists alongside traditional methods of communicating, offering more options for today's business workers.

- Understand the different types of communications that take place in business organizations.

- Understand how the Total Quality Management philosophy applies to communications and problem-solving skills.

- Identify key skills needed for quality telephone communications.

- Identify the personal qualities that contribute to a positive telephone persona.

Telecommunications Technology

The field of telecommunications is one of the fastest growing and fastest changing areas of technology today. **Telecommunications** is the linkage of telephone technology, computer technology, and transmission technology to send voice, text, graphics, and images from one location to another. Electronic **networks** are used to connect the different types of equipment needed to process data received in all these different forms and transfer it into a format that can be handled by the equipment at the other end. This means, for instance, that you can "talk to" a computer and have your words translated into a text format, or speak into a telephone receiver to dial a number instead of using the telephone keys. You can scan an image into a computer and have it show up on a television monitor, or have face-to-face telephone conversations via a videophone.

The telecommunications field is a growth area for job opportunities. There is the technical side that involves training in engineering, systems planning, systems implementation, administration and maintenance of telecommunications networks, and many other areas of specialization. There is also what might be called the end user or professional side of telecommunications that involves using the telephone, facsimile machines, voice mail systems, and electronic information systems to perform tasks in many different types of jobs. This latter

Figure 1-1

Excellent communication skills and understanding of telecommunications technology are essential for success in today's business world.

aspect of telecommunications technology and skills is the subject matter of this text. The central focus will be on the telephone, because it is the main instrument through which telecommunications is conducted.

411

Advancements in technology have historically earmarked the stages of our civilization's development. The invention of the desktop computer propelled us from the Industrial Age to the **Information Age.** Now we are entering a new era of technology known as the **Interactive Age.** We are already accustomed to **interactive technology,** which allows a user of a computer or telecommunications device to initiate an action to which the computer will respond. Computer games, automated teller machines, and automated telephone operators are just a few examples of the widespread use of this technology in the Information Age.

The Interactive Age will potentially bring a wide range of interactive technology into every home, with access through the television set. One potential service is called **infotainment**—a vast menu of information and entertainment—that subscribers can access on demand by pressing buttons on the TV remote control. Some examples of what users will be able to do include calling up catalogs to order products; contacting restaurants for menus, reservations, or home deliveries; viewing movies and entertainment programs at their convenience; and using references and information sources. The combined resources and talent of the giant telecommunications, entertainment, and technology companies are building **information warehouses, highways, and interfaces** that will store, transport, and access the interactive technology. The term **Information Superhighway** has been coined to refer to this entire system. According to a 1994 issue of *Newsweek* magazine, before the end of the decade technology companies will spend as much as $2 trillion building interactive infotainment systems.

THE COMMUNICATIONS PROCESS

The **communications process,** the act of sending information and receiving feedback, is a fundamental aspect of any business operation. Computer technology has made it possible to create, process, and distribute more information, in many different formats, at a faster pace than ever before.

In the past, most businesses relied on the written word and the first-class U.S. Postal Service as the primary means of exchanging information. Today, businesses rely heavily on the telephone, the fax machine, electronic mail systems, and electronic voice processing systems to move information and complete business transactions quickly and efficiently. However, it is important to note that technology has not completely replaced traditional methods of communicating and distributing information. What it has done is provide workers with a much broader range of options to consider when approaching communications tasks. The table below shows traditional methods and their Information Age counterparts.

Traditional Methods	Telecommunications Methods
• Letters/memos	• Telephone/fax/electronic mail
• Face-to-face selling	• Telemarketing
• Customer service representative	• Automated information system
• Group meetings/conferences	• Conference call/video teleconference
• Telephone operators	• Automated attendants
• Secretaries/answering machine	• Voice mail/voice message
• Office-to-office phone calls	• Car phones, mobile cellular phones, airphones

Figure 1-2

Technology has changed the way individuals and businesses handle communications.

A – Courtesy of AT&T Archives.
B – Courtesy of Compression Labs., Inc.

THE TELEPHONE AS A COMMUNICATIONS TOOL

The telephone, while no longer the only means of instantaneous communication and feedback, has become even more critical in business communications. This is because telephone lines and equipment are the tools that link different kinds of electronic technology. With telecommunications technology, basic telephone systems and telephone lines can be used to store and retrieve messages; transmit printed documents; access computerized data; hold conferences with many participants viewing and exchanging data; and interact with many different kinds of automated computer systems. Employees can now have business telephone calls forwarded automatically from the office to their homes or other locations. Calls can be placed and received from cars and airplanes, or even while walking down the street.

The telephone is used extensively in business for both internal and external communications. **Internal communication** is the communication that takes place among the workers employed by a business organization. Interaction with the company's customers, clients, suppliers, and other business associates outside the organization is called **external communication.** It is helpful to be aware of the distinctions between these types of situations.

Internal Communications

This internal network can be as small as a suite of offices on one floor of a building or as large as a multinational corporation with offices around the world. The size of the company and the type of business determine the kinds of business activities that are handled by telephone. Typical internal business communications include:

- Screening/forwarding telephone calls

- Requesting/providing information

- Giving/receiving instructions

- Scheduling meetings and appointments

- Discussing ongoing projects

One of the most important aspects of handling internal business communications is being able to differentiate between those types of communications which should be handled orally and those which should be put in writing. For example, a common procedure in business is to use the telephone to set up meetings or request information. The telephone call is then followed up with an electronic mail message or an interoffice memorandum. Following up in writing confirms the oral message and provides a record that cannot be disputed.

In very large companies, internal telephone communications may be the only form of communication you have with certain departments or workers within the company. In a large sales organization, for instance, you may communicate on a weekly basis with the sales assistant at a branch office to get sales figures. Though you might never come face-to-face with this coworker, through telephone communications, you can develop a good working relationship that will help you both do a better job.

External Communications

The frequency of external telephone communications and the types of business activities handled by telephone depends greatly on the position you have in the company. For example, if you are a telemarketing representative, a reservations representative, an administrative assistant, or a customer service representative, you would spend a great deal of time on the telephone. In jobs that require heavy telephone contact, the telephone call is a part of a series of job tasks that are required to complete a specific business transaction. Along with handling the oral part of the telephone call, your work might include follow-up tasks necessary for completing the business transaction, such as updating a computerized database record, completing forms, and distributing information to other departments by computer, fax, or interoffice mail.

Consider the job of Elsa Ortega, a reservations representative for a large hotel chain.

Elsa works in a large office with many other reservations representatives. She handles reservations information from individuals and travel agencies around the world, yet she never actually meets any of the people with whom she speaks on the phone. In many cases, Elsa is the first contact that people have with the hotel, so it is crucial that she sound professional and positive. It is also crucial that the information she takes from the customers is complete and is recorded accurately in the reservations database. Mistakes in hotel reservations can cause tremendous problems for business travelers and vacationers when they arrive at their destination.

What kinds of problems might customers encounter if Elsa makes a mistake when handling their hotel reservations?

_____

_____

_____

Jobs that involve external communications regularly or on a full-time basis include:

- Administrative assistant/secretary

- Receptionist/operator

- Reservations representative

- Customer service representative

- Telemarketing representative

Figure 1-3

When you handle telephone communications, it is important to project a positive attitude.

Regardless of your specific job, each time you handle external communications, you are engaged in public relations for your company. The image you project over the telephone will be the image that persons outside the company carry in their minds of the entire organization.

■ Communications Skills

To project the right image for your company, you need to be able to apply sound communications skills when handling both internal and external communications. It is important to develop the ability to establish good, well-balanced telephone relationships. You will need to learn how to project a positive and professional attitude, to be friendly, but not get too familiar, and to handle the substance of the communication in a way that meets your goals, the goals of the person on the telephone, and the goals of the company.

Technology has made communication a more complex function in business. More options mean that better decision-making skills are needed. Employees need a solid foundation in communications and problem-solving skills in order to handle communications in a way that reflects well on the company and enhances its relationships with its customers.

THE QUALITY APPROACH TO COMMUNICATION

The emphasis in business today is on quality—the production of quality products and the delivery of quality services to customers. In recent years, many companies have adopted the **Total Quality Management (TQM)** philosophy. This philosophy, which was to build the highly successful Japanese economy, is based on the concept that quality means meeting the needs of customers and considering those needs in everything a company does.

The Total Quality Management philosophy recognizes the needs of customers, employees, and management, but places customer needs first.

Needs of the Customer

■ To have their demands, needs, and desires met in a timely and convenient manner at a reasonable cost.

■ To feel appreciated, needed, and respected by the company as a whole and by those individual employees with whom they come in contact.

■ To have confidence in the company and the belief that if something goes wrong, it will be corrected.

Needs of the Employees

■ To have a clear understanding of their role in the company and feel that management has reasonable expectations.

■ To have the tools and training necessary to do their jobs effectively and to get positive results—satisfy customer needs; satisfy the expectations of management; receive compensation and recognition for functioning well.

■ To feel that they have a voice in company policies and decisions and to be treated as responsible contributors to the achievement of the company's goals.

Needs of Management

■ To function in the most efficient and cost-effective way possible by having a well-trained, productive, and cooperative workforce.

- To understand the marketplace and compete effectively by delivering quality goods, services, and information in a timely manner and at a reasonable cost.

- To cultivate customer loyalty by projecting a positive image of quality, caring, and service.

To balance the needs of the company, the employees, and the customers requires employers to continually review and revise their procedures and processes. One good example of how these needs must be balanced is the widespread use of voice mail systems.

Whereas secretaries used to screen calls, many businesses now insist that all employees answer their own telephones. Most companies have downsized (cut staff), and no longer have secretaries for every one or two professionals. Computerized messaging systems, called **voice mail**, leave personalized messages, take orders, and perform other functions that used to be done by people. Some communications experts feel that these systems are being overused and that companies are losing the value of personal contact in order to make their operations more efficient.

BASIC COMMUNICATION AND PROBLEM-SOLVING SKILLS

The changes brought about by communications technology and new management approaches place more responsibility on the individual worker. The quality of your communication with others is essential to your success and the success of the company you work for. Consider this conversation between Juan, a telemarketing representative, and a customer:

Juan: Monarch's Order Department. How may I help you?
Customer: I would like to place an order from your fall sale catalog.
Juan: I'm sorry. I couldn't quite make out what you said.
Customer: Oh, could it be my accent? I'm from France.
Juan: No, you speak English very well. I think there's some interference on the line. May I have your number? I'll call you back immediately.
Customer: Of course. It's (718) 555-9352.
Juan: I could barely hear you. Was that (718) 555-5362?
Customer: No, it's 9352.
Juan: 9352. Okay, I'll call you right back.
Customer: Fine. Thanks.

No actual business has been transacted during this conversation. Yet, Juan has helped the company by creating a positive impression on a customer. Explain why this is so:

_____

_____

_____

When you communicate on the telephone, you use basic communications skills that can be easily taken for granted. After all, talking on the telephone is something that everyone does regularly. However, telephone communications in a business setting is very different from social conversation. Some of the skills that you will apply when conducting business include:

Organization. Organizing your work so that telephone calls are planned in advance and information is readily available when needed during a telephone call.

Time Management. Using time-management skills to schedule outgoing calls when they can best be completed without interruption and to balance incoming calls with other job priorities.

Speaking. Speaking clearly, at a pace that is comfortable for the listener, and in a well-modulated tone. Projecting a positive attitude and competence in handling the job.

Listening. Listening actively by focusing concentration on the telephone call and providing appropriate feedback to the other party.

Writing. Taking notes and messages accurately; taking the time to confirm numerical data and other information to ensure accuracy and completeness.

Problem-Solving. Using good judgment to handle problem situations and angry callers; being able to respond quickly, but not impulsively; acting with discretion and handling confidential information appropriately.

YOUR TELEPHONE PERSONA

The way you apply the basic skills that make you a competent communicator is reflected in your **telephone persona.** A persona is an individual's social facade or front; that is, the personality that is projected when playing a particular role in life. When you handle telephone communications for a company, you are, in effect, playing a role—the role of company representative. Therefore, your telephone persona may not necessarily reflect your true feelings. The feelings it should reflect are those of a company that is glad to hear from the caller, eager to help, and empathetic to the caller's needs. It would not be natural to actually feel this way all the time, and that is why you must consciously adapt a positive telephone persona.

In future chapters, you will learn more about the factors that can influence your telephone persona and how to handle specific problems, such as angry callers, a hectic work schedule, or distractions that take place around you. Some elements of your telephone persona that you will learn more about are:

Voice Tone and Quality. The voice quality should be pleasant, clear, and loud enough for the caller to hear. The tone of voice should be sufficiently varied so that it is not boring—it is difficult to pay attention to someone who speaks in a monotone. Conversely, your tone should never reach extremes on the phone. A voice that becomes too high or shrill can be painful for a listener. A voice that becomes too deep can be inaudible.

Attitude. Although people at the other end of the phone cannot see your facial expressions or body language, they can get a fairly good idea of how you are feeling from your voice. If you are bored, annoyed, or distracted, this comes through loud and clear at the other end of the line, even when your words are appropriate. Learning to sound upbeat and interested, even when you are having a bad day, is crucial to developing a positive telephone persona.

Image. By what you say and how you say it, you will project an image in the mind of the person on the other end of the telephone. The image you want to project is one of competence, professionalism, and friendliness. How formal or informal an image you present is dependent in many ways on the position you hold and your relationship with callers. When handling calls from people you work with regularly, for instance, you would adopt a friendlier, more relaxed manner than if you were screening calls for a top executive.

Competence. The qualities previously listed will not make you a successful communicator unless they are combined with competence in handling your job. To handle telephone communications competently, you will need to acquire a sound understanding of not only your specific job, but also of the company you work for and the type of business it conducts. If you work for a small company, it is easy to get to know the business, the people involved, and what they each contribute to the organization. Small companies frequently involve their employees in more than one aspect of the business, which makes it easier for them to respond to various communications needs.

Figure 1-4

An employee's telephone persona may be the only opportunity a company has to form a good relationship with customers.

In large companies, work tends to be more compartmentalized, and it is sometimes a challenge to figure out the structure of the company and the responsibilities of different departments and work groups. When you join a company, large or small, you should make an effort to understand where you fit into the big picture. In doing so, you will find out how your role in handling communications is an important part of the company's strategy for success.

As you study the remaining chapters in this text, you will gain more in-depth knowledge about the topics touched on in this chapter. You will learn about telecommunications equipment—it's features, functions, and how it is used in different business settings. You will study standard business procedures and protocol for making and receiving telephone calls and how to handle international calls. And you will learn about the types of jobs that require telecommunications skills and how you can master the tasks required to be successful in the career you choose.

◼ Chapter Summary

◼ Telecommunications is the linkage of telephone technology, computer technology, and transmission technology to send voice, text, graphics, and images from one location to another via electronic networks.

◼ Technology has created many new options for communicating and distributing information. In addition to traditional telephone calls, options include the fax machine, electronic mail, voice processing, and information processing systems.

◼ The telephone is still the basic communications tool in business. Basic telephone systems can be used to store and retrieve messages, access computerized data, forward calls, hold conferences, and interact with automated systems.

◼ Internal communication takes place among the workers employed by a business organization; external communication involves interaction with customers, suppliers, and others outside the organization.

◼ The Total Quality Management philosophy emphasizes the needs of the customer in every aspect of a business organization's operations.

◼ Important skills for success in business are the basic communications skills—speaking, listening, and writing—as well as problem-solving, organization, and time-management skills.

◼ It is important to project a positive, competent, and professional telephone persona at all times when conducting business over the phone.

◼ Key Terms

communications process
external communication
Information Age
Information Superhighway
information warehouses, highways,
    and interfaces
infotainment
Interactive Age

interactive technology
internal communication
network
telecommunications
telephone persona
Total Quality Management
    (TQM)
voice mail

Chapter Review

Write your answers to the questions that follow and be prepared to discuss them in class.

1. **Why is the telephone the basic communications tool in business?**

   _____

   _____

   _____

   _____

2. **Face-to-face selling is the traditional method for generating sales with customers. What is the comparable telecommunications method of selling? List two advantages and disadvantages of each method.**

   _____

   _____

   _____

   _____

3. **In addition to speaking and listening, what four other skills are necessary for successful telephone communications? What problems might occur if an employee lacks some of these skills?**

   _____

   _____

   _____

   _____

   _____

4. **In the Total Quality Management approach to business, what is the primary need that must be met in order for a business to be successful? Explain why.**

5. Name three jobs that involve heavy telephone contact. List some advantages and disadvantages of such jobs.

_____

_____

_____

_____

_____

6. It is 1974 and O'Connell Construction, a large building contract company located in Pittsburgh, is in the process of preparing a bid for a new business center complex in downtown Tempe, Arizona. The bid must be mailed by the end of the business day if it is to be sure of arriving in Arizona on time. Everyone in the company is working hard to get the bid completed. Secretaries are keying and rekeying different sections of the bid, while constantly being interrupted by ringing phones. Managers are on the phone with subcontractors, taking down long, detailed lists of information. One executive needs to discuss the changes to the building schedule with three different managers who are all out of the office. He will have to wait until they call in. By mid-afternoon he has spoken with two of the managers, repeating the same things in each call. The third manager is on a plane to California, so he cannot be reached until late evening. At 4 p.m., the executive in charge is trying to face the fact that they are going to miss the deadline and probably lose out on the contract. The telephone plays an important part in this scenario. How might telecommunications technology change this scene if it were happening today? Share ideas with members of your class.

_____

_____

_____

_____

Read the background information below. Then turn on your audiocassette player and listen to Audio Dialogue 1-1. Consider the basic communications skills discussed in the chapter as you listen (organization, time management, speaking, listening, writing, and problem-solving), and evaluate each of the participants in the conversation in light of these skills. Turn off the player when the end of the dialogue is announced. (Do not rewind the cassette.) Then answer the questions below.

Background: George Willis owns a new sporting goods store. He wants to buy advertising time on a local all-sports radio station, and he wants to use a commercial that he has already used on other stations. He has written to the station asking for information concerning the cost of advertising time for his favorite show.

Mark Hammond sells advertising time on KSPT and has received Mr. Willis's letter. He sends a letter to Mr. Willis with information on costs for all the shows on the station. In addition, he decides to call with a response to Mr. Willis's questions.

Audio Analysis 1-1

1. As the caller, does Mark Hammond seem organized and prepared for his conversation with Mr. Willis? Explain your answer.

2. Do you think Mark Hammond is a good listener? Explain your answer.

3. Do you think George Willis is a good listener? Explain your answer.

4. Would either Mr. Willis or Mr. Hammond have benefited from taking notes during the conversation? Explain who you think would have benefited and why you think so.

_____

_____

_____

_____

5. Did either Mr. Willis or Mr. Hammond exhibit problem-solving skills during the conversation? Explain who exhibited these skills and give examples.

_____

_____

_____

_____

6. In your opinion, what else, if anything, could Mark Hammond have done to close the sale during the call? Explain your answer.

_____

_____

_____

_____

COMMUNICATIONS SYSTEMS AND EQUIPMENT

On the Job:
A Sampler of Communications Options

Monica Fernandez is the executive assistant to the marketing director of Westbrook Realtors, a commercial real estate firm. It is Monday morning and the first thing Monica wants to get out of the way is a couple of tasks left over from last week's planning of the company's annual awards banquet.

The first thing she has to do is notify the sales staff of the date, time, and place of the banquet. To do this she calls the voice messaging system and sends a message to all the marketing representatives, who are located in various offices throughout the region. She is able to record one message and send it simultaneously to all 50 of the company's reps. In case any of them neglect to pick up their voice mail messages, she also faxes a memo to each person. She can access a number that is programmed to transmit a copy of the memo to all of the representatives with one press of a button.

Next, she needs to approve the final design of the sculpture that is being created for the awards. She calls the manufacturer and turns on her videophone monitor. Bill Gibson, the manufacturer's representative, displays the sculpture in front of the videophone camera lens so that Monica can see that it meets the agreed upon design specifications. While Monica is looking at the sculpture, Bill faxes her a printed copy of the text that will be engraved on the awards. He points to the place on the sculpture where the engraved plate will be placed. Monica reads and approves the text, signs her approval of both the text and sculpture, and faxes the document back to Bill.

Monica has used the latest telecommunications technology to complete in less than half an hour two tasks that might ordinarily have taken days.

This is an example of some of the most advanced technology available to businesses today. While you may not encounter this level of sophistication on the job, you will undoubtedly use communications equipment other than just the telephone. You need to be familiar with the kinds of communications equipment and services used in business, as well as the systems and procedures that are available for handling incoming and outgoing telephone calls.

Objectives

After completing this chapter, you should be able to:

- Identify the different types of systems and procedures used by businesses to handle incoming and outgoing telephone calls.

- Recognize how technology has expanded the options available for handling internal and external communications in business.

- Identify different types of telephone equipment and explain how the available features serve a variety of business needs.

- Understand how telecommunications technologies such as facsimile transmission, voice processing, and teleconferencing are used in business.

■ Communications Systems

Companies have different kinds of systems and procedures for handling telephone communications. The traditional method, which is rarely used, is to have a centralized staff of operators who answer all incoming calls. The calls are then transferred to the appropriate department where they are answered by a secretary or receptionist. He or she directs the call to the appropriate executive or professional or takes a message. Some small to medium-sized companies hire one or more receptionists to answer and direct all incoming calls in a similar manner.

In recent years, the combination of factors that you read about in Chapter 1 —downsizing of staff, new technology, and an emphasis on quick and direct customer service—has brought about changes in the way company communications systems are organized. While centralized systems still exist today, they are used in combination with decentralized systems. Callers have the option of direct telephone access to individuals without going through a transfer process. Managers recognize that it is more time- and cost-effective, as well as more customer-oriented, to have individuals answer their own telephone lines.

CENTRALIZED SYSTEMS

It is necessary for most companies to have a centralized answering system from which all departments and individuals in the company can be reached. The central system is accessed by dialing a general number, often an 800 (toll-free) number. This number may be answered by an operator who switches the call to the individual, department, or extension number requested, or it may be answered by an automated attendant.

An **automated attendant** is a recorded message that directs calls through a computerized system. It provides a menu that lets a caller select from various options by pressing symbols, letters, or digits on the telephone keypad, or speaking one of the menu options. The system is programmed to direct the call to the appropriate individual or department, or to play additional recorded messages.

To access an automated attendant, the caller must have a **Touch-Tone™ telephone.** This is a telephone with buttons whose individual "tones" activate digitized pulses that can be interpreted by a computer program. **Rotary telephones,** which use a dial method of entering numbers and letters, cannot access the menu options on an automated attendant. If there is no speaking option, callers must select the option that puts them in touch with the operator. Most modern telephones have a Touch-Tone™/rotary switch. Following is an example of how an automated attendant works:

You have reached the Institute for Technology Training. If you know the extension of the person you are calling, dial it now. If you do not know the extension number, you may enter the person's last name followed by the first name now. If you need assistance, dial 0 for an operator.

For the next two weeks, keep a record of any telephone calls you make that are answered by an automated attendant. Make notes about the following and be prepared to discuss them with the class:

1. Did the attendant offer an option that was specific to your needs?

_____

_____

2. Did you feel that the automated system handled your call quickly and efficiently? Why or why not?

_____

_____

3. Did you experience any frustration due to the way your call was handled? If so, what could the company have done better?

_____

_____

Automated attendants can be a great convenience to both the caller and to the company. It is important, though, that the system be programmed to offer the menu options that meet customer needs. Callers sometimes become frustrated by automated attendants, particularly when they have to listen to a long list of options or are confused about which option to select. Long-distance callers sometimes complain that they are charged for time spent listening to information they don't need. And, of course, there are people who simply don't like "talking to a computer." It is up to the managers of a company to make sure that automated systems meet their callers' needs. In today's business world, however, most callers have become accustomed to this new technology and are able to adjust to not being greeted by "a live person."

DECENTRALIZED SYSTEMS

Decentralized communications systems are known as **direct dial.** These systems automatically direct incoming calls to extension numbers connected to a central exchange number. The **exchange** is the first three digits of the telephone number of everyone on the system. Internal calls can be made on the system by dialing only the last three or four digits, which is the **extension**

number. Each extension number is on a separate line. External incoming calls can be transferred from one line to another and they can be programmed to automatically "roll over" to another line if the extension that was dialed is busy.

A direct dial system makes it convenient for individual employees and groups of workers to handle their telephone calls in the way that best suits their needs and the needs of their callers. To make external calls, individuals simply have to press 9 and then dial as they would from any telephone. There are several procedures for handling incoming calls through a direct dial system.

Individual Pickup

Each employee has a personal extension number on a single-line or multi-line telephone on his or her desk. Employees answer all calls that come in to their personal telephone numbers and can pick up calls for others from their own telephone.

Sometimes there is a secretary or receptionist who has a **call director,** a telephone with buttons for all the extensions within the department or work group. When an employee's phone is not picked up after two or three rings, the secretary answers it and takes a message.

Figure 2-1

A single-line tele-phone is convenient for individuals on a direct dial system.

Figure 2-2

Multi-line tele-phones have buttons for each extension number on the sys-tem.

Courtesy of AT&T Archives.

Figure 2-3

A call director is used in a centralized system where an operator or receptionist answers and screens incoming calls.

Screening

The call is answered by a secretary or receptionist, who finds out who is calling and the purpose of the call before forwarding it to the appropriate executive or professional. This person may answer for one individual or a group of individuals. The secretary or receptionist is also responsible for handling routine telephone tasks, such as requests for information or products, and making sure that all messages are complete and accurate.

Many business telephones have a calling number display built into the telephone set. This displays the phone number of external callers and the name and phone number of internal callers, in effect, allowing the call to be screened without the intervention of a secretary.

Voice Mail

The two systems described previously may be augmented by a voice mail system. Instead of having the secretary or receptionist pick up when an individual is away from his or her telephone, a greeting, usually recorded by the individual, answers and requests that the caller leave a message. Voice mail greetings can be easily altered to fit the situation. For instance, a greeting that says, "I am away from my desk," when an employee is in the office, can be easily changed to, "I will be out of the office July 23 and July 24," when the employee goes on a business trip.

In many offices, all employees are on the voice mail system. This ensures that no calls are missed and that callers feel assured that their message is being received and handled in a timely manner. A typical greeting from a professional who is away on a business trip might say:

Hello, this is Globe Advertising. You have reached the office of Kimberly Jackson, product manager. I will be out of the office on November 18, 19, and 20. Please leave a message and I will return your call as soon as I get back. If you need immediate assistance, please contact my assistant, Leslie Abrams, at 555-2345.

With voice mail, callers can feel free to leave personalized and detailed messages. Often, this saves time by eliminating the need to return calls and it reduces **telephone tag,** the continual exchange of messages without the callers being able to make direct contact with each other.

Telephone Equipment

Basic telephone equipment has not changed much in recent years, but the many electronic communications options available today have created a competitive market for equipment manufacturers. The greatest enhancement to basic telephone equipment has been the invention, through use of technology, of features that support the communications needs of businesses and consumers. Many of these features come with basic telephone service; other optional features are available for a small monthly charge.

STANDARD EQUIPMENT AND FEATURES

Standard equipment comes with built-in features such as a hold button. A redial feature and abbreviated dial program have also become standard features on most telephones. Optional features, which are programmed into the system by the service provider, can be activated by entering a code, which is a combination of symbols and digits, such as *7. Some basic and optional features include:

Hold. A button which temporarily suspends the caller while waiting for someone to pick up the line or while information is being acquired. Phone systems can be programmed to play music or make announcements to callers while they wait.

Call Waiting. A sound that signals that a second call is coming in while a caller is on the line. The person receiving the call can ask the first caller to hold, quickly push and release the disconnect button, and answer the second call.

Call Forwarding. The ability to automatically forward incoming calls from one number to another.

Call Transfer. The ability to transfer calls from one telephone line to another without going through an operator.

Intercom. An internal line which allows two or more people within the office to speak to one another without using the outside telephone lines.

Conferencing. The ability to place calls to three or more parties simultaneously on one telephone line. Once everyone is on the line, all parties can take part in the conversation.

Abbreviated or Speed Dialing. Allows the caller to create codes for frequently called numbers, so that the numbers can be dialed by pressing only one or two digits.

Last Number Redial. A button on the telephone that, when pushed, automatically dials the last number that was dialed by the caller. This saves the time of reentering a number continually to call back when a busy signal is received.

Automatic Callback. Automatically redials a busy number once every minute or so, and signals with a ring when the call goes through.

Message Alert. A light which indicates that a voice mail message is waiting or a programmed voice that repeats the word "message" when the line is picked up.

Ring Designation. Rings that differentiate internal and external calls. For example, one long ring may signal internal calls and two shorter rings in quick succession may signal external calls.

Many telephones now also have electronic display features. These include:

Caller Identification (ID). Displays an incoming caller's phone number and the time and date of the call. Internal caller ID systems display the caller's extension number and name.

Call Record System. Shows the date, time, number called, and the length of each call. Printouts of calls can be obtained from a connected computer.

Multilingual Display. Displays data on incoming calls in several languages, usually English, Spanish, and French.

Figure 2-4

This telephone has an electronic display for caller identification.

Courtesy of Northern Telecom, Inc.

SPEAKERPHONES

Speakerphones may be desk phones or large-sized consoles that are used mainly for conferences. This equipment allows the user to speak and listen through an amplification system built into the telephone without using the handset. Larger systems can be used for conference calls where there are several participants in one location. Some of these are "intelligent" systems that can adapt to room acoustics, so all speakers can be heard without having to crowd around the equipment. These systems also can ensure that conversations sound fluid, without clipped syllables or cut-off phrases.

Figure 2-5

Speakerphones are usually used for business meetings where a group can sit around a desk or table and participate in a conference.

VIDEOPHONES

This is probably the most dramatic enhancement to telephone equipment since its invention. **Videophones** allow participants in telephone conversations to see each other via a video monitor. The equipment offered by major manufacturing companies, such as AT&T, works with existing jacks and telephones, and no additional service or equipment is needed. This equipment is now available at costs that are affordable for businesses and its use is expected to become more widespread in the near future. While the cost of videophone calls is no greater than regular calls, some communications experts predict that videophones will be used more for conferences than in one-to-one conversations. These experts feel that businesspeople do not necessarily want to look at each other while conducting routine telephone conversations.

Videophone features include:

- On-screen messages and prompts that remind the user when to press buttons.
- A self-view mode that allows the user to check his or her own image before and during a call.
- A one-way video mode that allows the user to opt not to be seen.
- Screen focus and brightness and image sharpness adjustments.

Privacy features include:

- No video image is transmitted until the video button is pressed.
- A manual shutter that physically blocks the camera lens when it is closed.
- A hold button that suspends both sound and video image.
- A mute button that silences the handset and speakerphone.

Figure 2-6

The videophone is a major technological breakthrough in telecommunications.

Courtesy of AT&T Archives.

Below list the advantages and disadvantages of using a videophone in business. After you have made your list, discuss it with members of the class to see where there is agreement and disagreement. What is the consensus of the class?

Advantages _____

_____

_____

_____

Disadvantages _____

_____

_____

_____

MOBILE TELEPHONE EQUIPMENT

Telephone equipment that can be used to conduct business while on the move has become a commonplace phenomenon. While out of the office, employees have many options for telephone communications other than the standard pay telephone. The most commonly used kinds of mobile communications devices are airphones, cellular phones, and pagers.

Airphones

Airphones are telephone systems that allow calls to be made from airplanes, both on the ground and in-flight. Callers can use a credit card to charge costs of calls. Some airlines provide airphones at the passenger's seat; others provide them at the front and back of the airplane.

Figure 2-7

Some airlines have telephones that can be accessed by the passenger.

© 1994 Northwest Airlines.

Cellular Phones

Cellular telephones are wireless phones that

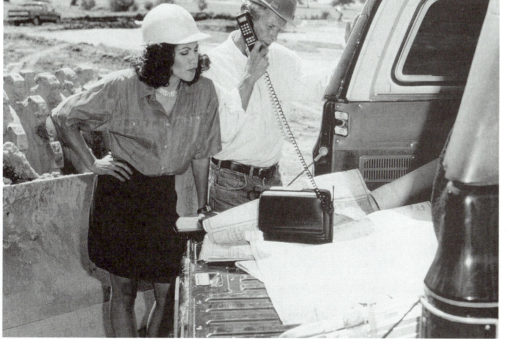

Figure 2-8

Cellular phones may be large, like this one, or small enough to carry in a pocket or briefcase.

Courtesy of Motorola Corporation.

operate through subscription to services that provide transmission from a network of stations. These stations use airwaves that are blocked out in "cells" within a particular region. The caller can move from one cell to another without disruption of the call, but if the range is too far, the call will "break up" and communication will be lost.

Pagers

Also called "beepers," these pocket-sized devices signal when a call is coming in to a user's designated number. The signal may be a sound (a beep) or a vibration that can be felt against the skin. The caller's number is shown on a digital display, and the user can contact the caller at the nearest telephone.

Telecommunications Technology

The integration of electronic equipment with telephone technology has created many options for immediate exchange of information. Facsimile transmission and voice processing are technologies that have been integrated with telephone technology and made available to the end user for handling a variety of situations. Office workers who have access to this communications technology are able to decide which option best suits the purpose of a specific communications task.

FACSIMILE TRANSMISSION

Basic facsimile transmission provides the ability to instantaneously transmit text and graphics over telephone lines. This technology has been around for a long time, but now it can be integrated with computerized telecommunications systems to provide a broad range of transmission options.

Facsimile (Fax) Machines

This basic equipment is used to transmit printed documents over telephone lines from one machine to another. Most offices have **dedicated lines,** which are lines used only for their facsimile transmissions. If a dedicated line is not available, facsimile transmissions and telephone transmissions can be conducted over the same telephone line. The facsimile machine is programmed to differentiate a telephone call from a fax transmission. When the phone rings, a tone indicates that a fax transmission is about to take place. If the call is picked up, the user can simply press a button that tells the fax transmission to start. If the call is not picked up, the machine automatically starts the transmission.

Like voice mail, fax machines allow users to send messages and information back and forth when one party is absent. Most offices can receive fax transmissions 24 hours a day.

Some features of sophisticated facsimile equipment include:

- The ability to store transmissions in case of power loss or paper outage.

- The ability to transmit incoming documents to alternate locations.

- Built-in security, including confidential mailboxes and restriction of unauthorized transmission or reception.

- The ability to program two or more fax numbers onto the same one-touch key—when the first number is busy, the second number is automatically dialed.

Figure 2-9

An example of a standard facsimile machine that is used in most office settings.

Photo by Alan Brown/Photonics.

Personal computers also have the ability to send and receive faxes. Some models are manufactured with a built-in fax transmission capability. Others require the addition of a fax board and an inexpensive software package.

Fax Attendant

A system which integrates voice mail and fax communications systems is called a **fax attendant.**

Incoming features include:

- Notification on the telephone message alert system of fax arrival.

- Confidential reception of fax messages.

- The ability to have faxes stored in voice mailboxes and have them delivered to a fax machine at a hotel or any other location, any time of the day or night.

Outgoing features include:

- A "broadcast" feature that allows one fax to be sent simultaneously to many people at different locations.

- The ability to enter fax numbers individually or via a special list stored in the system.

- A retry option that allows faxes to get through even if the receiving fax is busy or if the transmission is interrupted midstream.

Fax Response

An additional feature available with the fax attendant, a fax response system, lets callers request price lists, product descriptions, news—almost any type of information—and have it faxed to any fax machine 24 hours a day.

The fax response works as follows:

1. The caller dials a special fax response number and is offered a recorded menu of options.

2. After making a selection on a Touch-Tone™ phone, the caller enters the phone number of his or her fax machine.

3. The selected document is transmitted via fax to the caller's fax machine.

411

Fax technology has moved out of the office and is now available for businesspersons on the move. Rental car companies that offer car phones are adding fax machines. Many airlines are upgrading passenger seat phones to include fax capability, and some will allow faxing of short messages back to the ground. Large hotel chains, such as Ritz-Carlton and Sheraton, are offering electronic fax mailboxes with systems that allow faxes to be retrieved at additional locations designated by the guest, such as a client's office or the airport. The Spectrydyne service that is used by most hotels for computerized services to guest rooms, such as checking out and ordering room service, is now offering fax service via the television set. Using a television remote control, guests can read a fax and discard it or order it printed at the front desk.

VOICE PROCESSING

You have already learned about two types of voice processing technology, the automated attendant and voice mail. This technology is used to handle routine incoming calls. More sophisticated voice messaging systems and voice information systems are available for large customer service operations and other kinds of businesses that handle large volumes of incoming calls, such as hotels.

Voice Messaging Systems

These computerized systems come with software that can be modified to fit the specific needs of a company. They let the user send voice messages to one person or to a whole company. For instance, most large hotels have voice messaging systems that allow callers to leave recorded messages for guests, rather than speaking to an operator. Voice messaging systems can accommodate thousands of voice mailboxes, store and forward hundreds of messages, and manage high volumes of calls simultaneously.

Special features include:

- Personal mailboxes for people who share one telephone line.

- The ability to create multiple personal greetings that can be selected and deselected as needed.

- Prioritizing of messages, so that important messages, such as customer problems, are placed ahead of other messages.

- The ability to send messages out by name, number, or list to others on the system without calling each one individually.

- The ability to designate a specific date and time for messages to be sent to an individual or broadcast to a list of users.

Voice Information Systems

These systems are programmed for large-scale interactive transactions. They are used by companies such as banks, schools, retailers, and transportation companies, many of which offer 24-hour, seven-days-a-week services. Voice information systems can be programmed to provide virtually any information that requires simple selections from a caller. For instance, customers can get information on their financial balances or make payments; register for courses or get information on course offerings; get travel fare and schedule information; purchase tickets or buy subscriptions; or place orders for product purchases. These types of systems give consumers the ability to access information quickly and at their own convenience, as shown in the following example:

> Welcome to Universal Credit Union. If you know the extension of the person you wish to reach, please dial it now. For account information, teller transactions, or loan payments, press 1. For loan information or to apply for a loan, press 2. For VISA account information, to apply for a VISA, or to report a card lost or stolen, press 3. For savings rates, CD rates, or new account information, press 4. For other information or if you are unsure, please press 0 for an operator.

Some voice information systems have speech recognition capabilities. They can recognize standard vocabulary consisting of digits zero (or "oh") through nine, and "yes" and "no." They can also translate computer-based text into clear, easy-to-understand computer-generated speech.

■ Teleconferencing

A teleconference is a meeting of three or more individuals or groups that takes place through telecommunications technology. The ability to hold meetings through teleconferencing technology has become more important than ever in today's business environment where employees are not necessarily located at one location. Teleconferencing allows businesses to save the cost of business travel and still have immediate interaction and feedback among key players in a business transaction.

Teleconferences usually employ basic telephone equipment for individuals and speakerphones when groups are involved. Computers and video equipment may also be used so that documents, charts, or other types of visuals can be shared among the participants in the conference.

On a basic telephone system, the conferencing feature can be accessed by pressing and releasing the disconnect button, by pressing a conference button or by entering a code. The caller can place calls to two or more different numbers and have all the parties speak on the same line. More sophisticated teleconferencing systems are used to conduct off-site meetings with large numbers of participants. These systems, called **teleconferencing bridges,** allow conference interaction regardless of geographic distribution or size of the groups participating. They also eliminate noises that sometimes occur over long-distance and multiple-line connections. The conferences are set up and monitored by an operator, called a **conference attendant,** who can control multiple conferences simultaneously.

Companies which do not have their own teleconferencing system can access these systems through the company that provides their local or long-distance telephone service. At a prearranged time, the conference attendant calls all participants and takes a "roll call" of attendance, once everyone is on the line. The attendant can monitor the call to identify poor connections and redial them without interrupting the rest of the conference. There is also a service called "Meet Me" that allows conferees to be notified in advance of the time of the call and to dial directly into the meeting.

Telephone Service Providers

Business telephone systems, services, and equipment are purchased through local and long-distance carriers. **Local carriers** supply services within specified local calling regions. These calling regions include the caller's area code, for which a standard monthly charge is assessed, as well as designated area codes within the region, for which the carrier assesses additional charges.

Long-distance carriers supply all services beyond the local calling area. Long-distance service is a highly competitive market, with AT&T, MCI, and Sprint being the market leaders. These companies offer a variety of service options to both their consumer and business customers. They also manufacture equipment that is compatible with the services they offer, as well as work with business customers to customize the computerized communications systems described in this chapter.

Chapter Summary

- Most businesses use a combination of centralized and decentralized systems to handle incoming telephone calls.

- Centralized systems are answered by an operator or an automated attendant, which is a recorded message that directs calls by giving the caller a choice of options that are activated by pressing the symbols, numbers, or letters on a Touch-Tone™ telephone.

- Decentralized systems use direct dial to route calls directly to individuals who can opt to answer their own telephones or have their calls screened by a receptionist or secretary.

- Voice mail is a computerized messaging system that is answered by a recording. Callers can leave a personal message in an individual's voice mailbox. The system stores messages until they are accessed by the person assigned to the mailbox.

- There are many standard and optional features available for basic telephone equipment. These include features built into the equipment, such as hold, speed dialing, transfer, and redial. Other features, such as call waiting, call forwarding, and conferencing, are made available through the telephone service provider.

- Electronic display features available on telephone equipment include caller identification, call record systems, and multilingual display.

- Speakerphones may be desk phones or consoles. They are useful for conference calls or for situations where workers need both hands free.

- Videophones allow participants in telephone conversations to see each other via a video monitor. While it is expected that use of this equipment will grow dramatically as its cost decreases, some experts feel that individuals in business are not necessarily eager to embrace the concept of face-to-face telephone conversations.

- Facsimile technology is a fast-growing aspect of electronic communications. Facsimile transmission can be integrated with telephone, personal computer, and voice mail systems to provide a complete range of communications options.

- Voice messaging and voice information systems are computerized telecommunications systems that can be tailored to suit a company's size and business operations. These systems can handle large volumes of calls, such as hotel voice mail systems, and provide automated customer services, such as banking and ticket purchases.

- Teleconferencing systems are used to conduct multi-site meetings with large numbers of participants. A company may have teleconferencing capabilities as a part of its communication system, or arrange for teleconferencing through a local or long-distance carrier.

- Telephone service is provided by local and long-distance carriers. These companies offer a variety of telecommunications services and equipment to both consumer and business customers.

Key Terms

automated attendant
call director
code
conference attendant
dedicated line
direct dial
exchange
fax attendant

fax response system
local carrier
long-distance carrier
rotary telephone
teleconferencing bridge
telephone tag
Touch-Tone™ telephone

Chapter Review

Write your answers to the questions that follow and be prepared to discuss them in class.

1. **What are the advantages and disadvantages of an automated attendant? Describe how you feel about being greeted by an automated attendant instead of a "live person."**

2. **A caller listens to Kimberly Jackson's voice mail greeting (on page 21). Kimberly's greeting does not ask for any specific information. What specific information would you have asked callers to include in their messages?**

3. **Review the list of telephone features on pages 22-23. Make a list of the features that you think are essential for every business to have. Make a second list of the nonessential features. Arrange each list in order of most important to least important.**

4. **Which long-distance telephone carrier provides your home long-distance service? Explain why your household chooses to do business with this particular carrier.**

5. **You work for a small company that designs and manufactures novelty items, such as T-shirts and coffee mugs, that companies purchase to give away at trade shows and conferences. Five of the 20 employees in the company sometimes work in the office and sometimes work from home. Your manager and the two vice presidents are out of the office frequently meeting with customers. Two secretaries take messages for the staff and screen incoming calls when they are specifically requested to do so. Otherwise, all employees answer their own telephones.**

   Your manager wants to update the telephone system to take advantage of some of the new features and technology that are available. Write a short report suggesting which features and automated systems you think would be most beneficial to your company.

Audio Dialogue 2-1	Read the background information below. Then turn on your audiocassette player and listen to Audio Dialogue 2-1. Turn off the player when the end of the dialogue is announced. (Do not rewind the cassette.) Then answer the questions below.

Background: Your company, Family Publishers, has just installed a new automated attendant system. You are a customer service representative for the video publishing group. Your boss asks you to listen to and evaluate the recording.

Audio Dialogue 2-1	1. How many steps does the customer have to go through before placing the actual order? (You may need to listen to the tape again.)

How many steps are there in all to complete the order?

2. What advantages does this automated order system offer the customer?

3. What advantages does the system offer the company?

4. As a company service representative for Family Publishers, would you be satisfied with the system? Explain your answer.

_____

_____

_____

_____

5. What changes, if any, would you make to the system?

_____

_____

_____

_____

_____

BASIC TELEPHONE COMMUNICATIONS SKILLS

Chapter

3

On the Job: Communicating Effectively

Luanne Jenkins is receptionist and switchboard operator for ExecuSpace, Inc. ExecuSpace rents office space—not to companies, but to individuals. People rent the space for a variety of reasons: Many are self-employed and work out of their homes, but want to present a "company" image to their clients. They use the attractive office space to meet with clients, or they take advantage of the support services provided by ExecuSpace. Other people who use ExecuSpace offices may work for large companies that are head-quartered elsewhere. They use the offices when they are in town. Still others may be from companies in other countries.

Luanne must answer the phone and take messages for this great variety of people, many of whom are not in the office. How does she know how to answer the phone? Her switchboard is computerized. Each client has his or her own phone number. When that number is called, the switchboard computer screen shows which number is being called and the name of the company or client. Luanne has a list of clients and how they want their phone to be answered. She answers each call as a representative of a different company. For example:

Luanne: Good morning. Melaney Consulting.
Caller 1:   John Melaney please.
Luanne: I'm sorry. Mr. Melaney is not in at the moment. May I take a
            message?
Caller 1:   Yes, this is Katharine Lyons of Baskin Construction. Please
            ask Mr. Melaney to call me before three this afternoon.
Luanne: What is your number, please?
Caller l: (609) 555-3856.
Luanne: (609) 555-3856. You are Katharine Lyons of Baskin
            Construction, and you would like Mr. Melaney to call you
            before three this afternoon.
Caller 1:   Right. Thanks. Good-bye.

Luanne: Bye.

(Luanne calls Mr. Melaney at home and gives him the message.)

Luanne: Good morning. Tech-Time International. How may I help you?
Caller 2: Orlando Montoya, please.
Luanne: Mr. Montoya is in a meeting. May I take a message?
Caller 2: Yes, this is Maria Dominguez. I just wanted to tell Mr. Montoya
           that I will be catching the early flight, so I will be able to meet
           with him tomorrow morning after all. I'm leaving for the
           airport now.
Luanne: I'll give Mr. Montoya your message. Is there some way that he
           can reach you to confirm the meeting?
Caller 2: Yes. I'll be staying at the Hilton on Park Street. He can leave a
           message for me there.
Luanne: Okay, Ms. Dominguez, I'll tell Mr. Montoya that you are catch-
           ing the early flight so you will be able to meet with him tomor-
           row morning and that you're staying at the Hilton on Park
           Street.
Caller 2: Thank you. Good-bye.
Luanne: Good-bye.

In order for Luanne to function well in her job, she must have excellent communications skills. Communications skills are essential for using the phone effectively.

Objectives

After completing this chapter, you should be able to:

■ Send and receive effective and appropriate telephone communications.

■ Speak at an acceptable pace.

■ Modulate your voice and control your tone of voice.

■ Pronounce and enunciate words correctly.

■ Use correct grammar and the appropriate vocabulary in your telephone communications.

■ Be alert for and aware of regional or national expressions and accents that can create communications problems.

■ Exhibit an appropriate business attitude in your telephone communications.

■ Apply listening skills by focusing your attention and providing feedback.

■ Effective Communication

In order for communication to be successful, the sender and the receiver must both actively participate in the communications process. The sender must strive to make the message clear, focused, and precise. The receiver must be attentive and responsive. Both must be sure that the message is received as it is intended.

Communication over the telephone is more difficult than it is in person because the people involved cannot see each other. Nonverbal messages such as facial expressions and body language are lost when we speak on the phone. It is, therefore, a challenge to both the sender and the receiver to avoid miscommunication and misunderstandings when doing business over the phone.

HOW COMMUNICATION WORKS

Effective communication is more than one person sending a message and another person receiving it. Following are the steps in the communications process:

1. The sender formulates the message. The sender determines what ideas are to be conveyed and the most appropriate way to convey them (through language, examples, references to papers, etc.).

2. The sender sends the message.

3. The receiver receives the message.

4. The receiver assimilates the message. This means that the receiver thinks about what the sender has said in order to understand the message.

5. The receiver provides feedback. The receiver may rephrase what the sender has said or may ask questions.

6. The sender responds.

7. Feedback continues between sender and receiver until understanding and agreement is achieved.

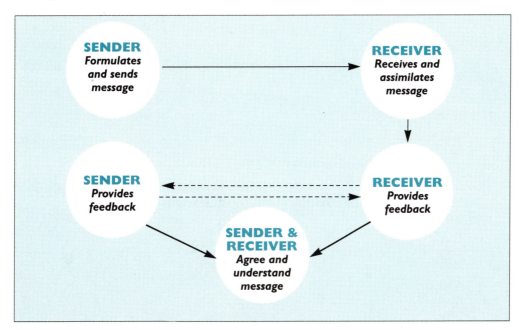

Figure 3-1

Diagram of Communication Process.

THE IMPORTANCE OF FEEDBACK

Regardless of who makes the call, both people involved in the conversation should provide **feedback**. It is only with feedback that both people can be assured that what they are saying is understood as it was intended to be. Do not end the call until important points are reviewed and agreed upon by both people.

If, for example, you are supposed to make hotel reservations for the person you are speaking with, repeat all the vital information before the call is ended. Following is an example:

McClintock:	So you'll be arriving in town the day before the meeting—the 27th.
Jeffers:	Yes, that's right.
McClintock:	I'll reserve a room for you at the Excelsior Hotel for the nights of the 27th and 28th. You'll be leaving on the morning of the 29th, right?
Jeffers:	Yes. I'll be flying in on the 3:15 p.m. flight on the 27th, and I'll be taking the 9:20 a.m. flight home on the 29th.
McClintock:	I'll have the hotel hold your reservation for late arrival.
Jeffers:	That's a good idea. I have your address, but I'll need the address of the hotel. Oh, what time will the meeting start?
McClintock:	We'll start at 9:15. The address of the hotel is 129 Liberty Avenue. Let me just make sure I have this right. You'll be arriving on the 27th of October. You'll be staying here for the nights of the 27th and 28th, and you'll be leaving on the 29th.
Jeffers:	That's everything. Let me confirm the information at my end. I'll be at the Excelsior Hotel, 125 Liberty Avenue.
McClintock:	No, that's 129 Liberty Avenue.
Jeffers:	129. The meeting starts at 9:15 on the 28th. And your address is 293 West Morgan.
McClintock:	Right. Oh, we're on the sixth floor.
Jeffers:	The sixth floor. OK. I'll see you on the 28th.

1. What problems might Jeffers have encountered if he had not repeated all the information?

_____

_____

_____

2. Other than providing feedback over the phone, what else can McClintock do to ensure that all the information about the meeting is communicated correctly?

_____

_____

_____

3. What should McClintock do if all the rooms at the Excelsior are booked for the nights in question?

_____

_____

_____

Notice how both people in the conversation provide feedback, and both can feel confident that the information they have is correct. McClintock should send a follow-up fax or letter after the hotel reservation is made. But even if he doesn't, Jeffers has enough information to get to the meeting without any trouble. This is because McClintock and Jeffers communicated well.

■ Avoid Distractions

Your attention is essential to effective communication. **Distractions** can be anything from looking through your mail while you are on the phone, to trying to do other work, to having someone in your office, to construction noise. As busy as you are and as tempting as it may be, do not try to do two things at once. Your inattention can lead to misunderstandings. It is also most likely apparent to the person at the other end of the line that your mind is elsewhere.

Figure 3-2

Interruptions while on the phone can lead to misunderstandings.

Most people in an office will not disturb someone on the phone. If people try to attract your attention while you are on the phone, wave them away. If they persist, ask the person on the phone to hold for a moment while you take care of what may be an urgent matter. If the matter at hand requires your immediate attention, ask the person on the phone whether it will be okay for you to call back. Find out when it will be most convenient, and be sure to call back when you say you will.

If the area in which you work is noisy and you have a door, close it when you are on the phone. The noise is not only a distraction to you, but it will likely be one to the person you are speaking with as well. If you do not have a door, try to schedule calls during the quieter periods of the day. If you have an extremely important call, it may be possible for you to make it from an empty office.

Speaking Skills

Your speaking skills can have a significant impact on your ability to communicate effectively. Because you are not face-to-face with the person you are speaking with, all you have is your voice, what you say, and how you say it to convey a message. A university study determined that 55 percent of the information we communicate is through body language; 38 percent is through voice inflection; and only 7 percent is through the content, or our words. Therefore, your voice and speech patterns are magnified in importance when you speak on the phone.

PACE

The rate, or **pace**, at which you speak can affect the listener's ability to understand you. If you speak too quickly, your words may run together and be difficult to comprehend. Too swift a pace may also make it difficult for the listener to take in everything that you say. On the other hand, if you speak too slowly, the listener may become bored or restless and his or her attention may wander.

People in certain regions of the United States are known to have either rapid or slow rates of speech. In parts of the Northeast, people are thought to speak quickly. In parts of the South, people are thought to speak slowly. Consider where you are from and where your listener is from, and try to pace yourself.

Regardless of where people are from, some people just naturally speak very quickly, while others naturally speak very slowly. If you are not sure whether you fall into one of these categories, ask someone you trust to tell you.

MODULATION

Some people naturally speak loudly; others speak softly. Extremes of either can be a problem over the phone. If you speak too loudly, it may hurt the ear of the listener. If you speak too softly, the listener will have to strain to hear you. If you are not sure whether you have either of these problems, ask a friend with whom you speak on the phone frequently.

Try to remember to **modulate**, or control the level of, your voice when you are on the phone. In addition, if you believe that you speak too softly, be sure to speak directly into the phone receiver. This will help your voice carry. If you believe you speak too loudly, hold the receiver slightly away from your mouth. This will help to make you sound less loud at the other end of the line.

TONE

The **tone** of your voice should be sufficiently varied so that it is not boring—it is difficult to pay attention to someone who speaks in a monotone. Conversely, your tone of voice should not reach extremes on the phone. A voice that becomes too high-pitched or shrill can be painful to the listener. A voice that becomes too deep can be inaudible.

Some people speak in a singsong voice in which the tone goes up and down in a repetitive pattern. This kind of tonal variation can be as annoying and as difficult to listen to as a monotone.

PRONUNCIATION

Correct pronunciation is an essential speaking skill. Mispronounced words can easily be misunderstood. And not only do they detract from effective communication, but they also reflect on you—your education and professionalism.

Words that are frequently mispronounced include:

Word	Correct Pronunciation	Common Mistake
statistics	sta-tis-tics	sa-tis-tics
ask	ask	ax
height	hite	hith
specific	spe-ci-fic	pa-ci-fic
library	li-brar-ee	li-berry

Some words may be pronounced correctly more than one way, such as harassment, vase, Caribbean, and Monaco. Decide how you wish to pronounce such words and be consistent. If you can't decide, consult a dictionary. The first pronunciation shown is the current preferred way.

ENUNCIATION

Enunciation is different from pronunciation in that pronunciation refers to *how* you say a particular word. Enunciation refers to how *clearly* you say a particular word. It is possible to pronounce a word incorrectly but to enunciate it well, and vice versa.

It is important that you speak clearly and distinctly. Don't compress or skip over syllables. For example, say "going to" instead of "gonna." Also, do not leave off the ends of words. For example, say "going to," not "goin' to."

GRAMMAR

As with mispronounced words, poor grammar is also a reflection of your education and your professionalism. Some rules of grammar are more relaxed when you speak than when you write. For example, you do not have to speak in complete sentences. You can use colloquial or occasional slang expressions. And you can use contractions. However, the fundamental rules of grammar apply whether you are speaking or writing. Following are some common errors:

Wrong	Right
between you and I	between you and me
he don't, she don't	he doesn't, she doesn't
Each person believes that they…	Each person believes that he or she…
Each of the members are present	Each of the members is present

VOCABULARY

Some people think that if they use long words, it will make them sound educated and knowledgeable. On the other hand, some people think that those who use lots of long words are pompous or show-offs. You can assume with certainty that if you use long words incorrectly or inappropriately, you will be viewed as under-educated or even foolish. It is always better to use a short word that you know the meaning of rather than a long word that you are unsure of.

By the same token, some people believe that if they hear a word with which they are unfamiliar and ask for the definition, they will appear ignorant or foolish. The opposite is often true: People who are confident and well-educated are willing to admit that they do not know something. If asking a customer or colleague to explain the meaning of a word to you makes you uncomfortable, try to determine the meaning through context and by rephrasing what has been said in terms with which you are comfortable. The back and forth feedback in your conversation will let you know whether you have figured out the meaning of the word in question.

LOCAL REGIONAL EXPRESSIONS

If you have lived, gone to school, and worked in only one region of the United States, you might assume that terms and expressions you use would be understood everywhere because you have no reason to assume otherwise. Although this is true for most of what you say, some expressions you use may be regional rather than national. Following are some examples of expressions that differ in different parts of the country:

oversleep	sleep in	
submarine sandwich	hero	hoagy
frank	frankfurter	hot dog
soda	soda pop	pop
pocketbook	purse	

If you find yourself in conversations with people from other parts of the country who ask you to repeat something that you've said, it may not be because they couldn't hear you. It may be because they are not familiar with an expression you have used.

Audio Dialogue 3-1

Read the background information on the following page. Then turn on your audiocassette player and listen to Audio Dialogue 3-1. Turn off the player when the end of the dialogue is announced. NOTE: This dialogue is in two parts. Do not turn off the player after the first part. (Do not rewind the cassette.) Then answer the questions on the following page.

Background: Christie Raymond handles reservations and special arrangements for business groups for the L & P Ranch, a hotel/resort in Wyoming. In addition to vacationers, the ranch can accommodate small business conferences and meetings. She has been working with Ben DeLucca, who works for Science Software, a small, but successful, software development company located in New York City. Ben has only recently joined the company. He is assistant manager of marketing services and has been assigned the task of coordinating plans for his company's annual sales meeting.

Audio Analysis 3-1

1. Once Christie realized that she had used an expression her customer was unfamiliar with, do you think she handled the situation well? Explain.

_____

_____

2. Do you think it was necessary for Ben to apologize to Christie about not knowing something? Explain. Why do you think he did so?

_____

_____

3. Do you know any expressions that are unique to your part of the country? Start compiling a list.

_____

_____

4. The dialogue mentions New York steak, French toast, and English muffins. List other foods whose names identify the place where they originated.

_____

_____

NATIONAL EXPRESSIONS

Many expressions are likely to be known and understood throughout the United States, but not by people from other countries, who may have learned English in school, where the language taught is usually quite formal. Even people from English-speaking countries such as England or Australia may be unfamiliar with some American expressions.

For example, don't tell someone from England that you will "go the whole nine yards" on a project, since this is a reference to American football and may be unfamiliar to people in other countries. Say, instead, that you will go all the way on a project. By the same token, do not ask someone from the Netherlands for a ballpark estimate (a reference to baseball). Ask for a rough estimate instead.

Many American expressions are derived from sports, such as the two examples cited above. Can you think of any others? Compile a list of sports-related idioms.

Figure 3-3

International communication is enhanced through the use of satellite links.

ACCENTS

Have you ever gone to a movie in which the characters spoke with foreign accents? After the movie you discussed it with your friends and found that some had no trouble understanding the accent while others complained that they could not understand what was being said. Some people have "an ear" for languages, including accents, while others struggle to understand.

Most people in the United States have some degree of a regional accent although they may not be aware of it if they are surrounded by people with the same accent. Some accents in the United States are considered more difficult to understand than others. These include accents from the South, the Northeast, and southwestern states such as Texas or Oklahoma. If you are from one of these areas and must speak with people from other areas, be sure to enunciate clearly so that you will be understood.

If you are from another country and have an accent, it is especially important that you speak slowly and enunciate well.

AUDIBLE AND VERBAL DISTRACTIONS

The distractions discussed earlier in this chapter concern things that may distract your attention. However, there are some distractions that are annoying and may have a negative effect on the person you are speaking with. For example, eating or chewing gum while you are on the phone creates an audible distraction. The sound of someone inhaling and exhaling smoke from a cigarette can also be an audible distraction for the listener, as can breathing directly into the receiver or shuffling papers.

You may have certain habits in your speech that can distract a listener. Do you frequently say "well," "like," or "you know"? These expressions may be less distracting in person than they are over the phone where the focus is solely on what you are saying. You may not be aware that you have repetitive speech habits. Listen to yourself carefully and try to avoid overuse of meaningless expressions.

ATTITUDE

Although people at the other end of the phone cannot see your facial expressions or body language, they can get a fairly good idea of how you are feeling from your voice. If you are bored, annoyed, or distracted, this comes through loud and clear at the other end of the line even though you have responded appropriately and have been polite. On the other hand, if you have a smile on your face, it is reflected in your voice.

You may be the first or only contact with your company that someone from the outside has. Therefore, that person's impression of you reflects on both you and your company. It is critical that you sound positive, interested, and sincere, even if you are having a bad day, are overwhelmed with work, or dislike the person at the other end of the phone.

Figure 3-4

Always have a positive, sincere attitude when you speak on the phone.

Communication works two ways. As the speaker, you have the responsibility to be clear, precise, and understandable. As the listener, you have responsibilities as well. You must listen actively by focusing your attention and providing feedback.

FOCUS YOUR ATTENTION

It is more difficult to pay attention to someone on the phone than it is in person. One reason for this is that you have nothing to look at that relates directly to the conversation. Although you may refer to correspondence or the contents of a file, you will not constantly look at these. If your eyes begin to wander, you may easily become distracted by other work on your desk or by something that is happening in the office. One way to avoid this problem is to make notes as you listen. You may want to jot down important points in the conversation or questions you want to ask when the opportunity presents itself. Not only does note-taking help you stay focused, but it also helps in the feedback process.

PROVIDE FEEDBACK

Feedback is discussed earlier as an integral part of the communications process. It generates discussion and eliminates potential misunderstandings or misinformation. Practice providing feedback until it becomes a natural part of your professional telephone personality.

HANDLE DIFFICULTIES

Many of the issues you must deal with as a speaker (pace, modulation, pronunciation, enunciation, accents, regionalisms, etc.) can confront you from the other side of the conversation as a listener. Since your responsibility as a listener is to be sure that you understand the message being sent, you cannot allow problems that affect your understanding to interfere with communication. You can ask someone to speak louder, to repeat something you missed, and to explain something you didn't understand. In this way, you will contribute to effective communication.

Chapter Summary

- Effective communication requires that (1) the sender formulates and sends the message, (2) the receiver gets and assimilates the message, and (3) the receiver provides feedback.

- Communication requires the undivided attention of the sender and receiver of messages; hence, avoid distractions while talking on the phone.

- Because you cannot see the person you are communicating with when you are on the phone, voice and speech patterns are especially important.

- The rate at which you speak should be neither too fast nor too slow.

- Your voice should not be too loud or too soft (modulation), and your tone should be varied and interesting.

- How you say words or expressions (pronunciation) and how clearly you say words or expressions (enunciation) affect your ability to communicate well.

- The vocabulary you use when communicating can be considered a reflection of your education and professionalism.

- Avoid expressions that may be local to your region of the country (or to the United States, if you are speaking to someone from another country). If you have an accent, be sure to speak clearly and distinctly.

- Present a positive, interested, and sincere attitude.

- As a listener, focus your attention and provide feedback.

Key Terms

distractions
enunciation
feedback
modulation
pace
pronunciation
tone

Chapter Review

Write your answers to the questions that follow and be prepared to discuss them in class.

1. **Is receiving a message on voice mail a true form of communication? Explain why or why not.**

_____

_____

_____

_____

_____

2. **Explain the difference between pronunciation and enunciation.**

_____

_____

_____

_____

_____

3. **Explain why not being able to see the person you are speaking with on the phone can affect communication.**

_____

_____

_____

_____

_____

4. **Does speaking very slowly present a problem to effective communication? Explain why or why not.**

_____

_____

_____

5. As a participant in a telephone communication, you are the speaker and the listener at different times during the conversation. Name two issues that can affect you as speaker and as listener. Explain how to deal with them as a speaker. As a listener.

_____

_____

_____

_____

_____

Read the background information below. Then turn on your audiocassette player and listen to Audio Dialogue 3-2. Turn off the player when the end of the dialogue is announced. (Do not rewind the cassette.) Then answer the questions below.

Audio Dialogue 3-2

Background: Service Hardware is a midsize hardware company in Michigan. The company has several retail stores in the state and takes catalog orders from around the country. Service recently acquired an 800 number, and its catalog business has increased as a result. In order to accommodate the additional business, Service has added John Taylor to its telephone staff. John is a native of Michigan. He has been through the company's training program and has been on the job for a week.

I. John Taylor almost lost an order for his company when he told the customer that Service didn't carry what the customer was asking for. How should John have responded when he realized that he did not understand what the customer was saying?

Audio Analysis 3-2

_____

_____

_____

_____

_____

2. Did the customer seem prepared to place the order? What might he have done differently?

_____

_____

_____

_____

_____

3. Do you think the training that Service Hardware gave John adequately prepared him for the job? Explain your answer.

_____

_____

_____

_____

_____

_____

4. Was there sufficient feedback between John and the customer? Explain.

_____

_____

_____

_____

_____

RECEIVING AND MAKING CALLS

On the Job: Handling Incoming and Outgoing Calls

Bob Donnelly is a sales assistant in the southern regional sales office of a large pharmaceutical company. Bob receives a steady stream of calls daily from sales representatives who need information or promotional materials. He also makes many calls to reps and to the marketing and sales managers at the company headquarters in New Jersey. For example:

Bob: Samler Pharmaceuticals. Bob Donnelly speaking.

Josie: Hi, Bob. This is Josie Laker in Atlanta.

Bob: Hi, Josie. What can I do for you?

Josie: I've arranged a video presentation of Cardilon with several VIPs at Langston Memorial Hospital for this Thursday. I tried to review the videotape last night, but I found that a big, black band went right through the middle of the screen. It's there for the whole tape. I can't possibly use it the way it is. Can you express me another tape?

Bob: We sent out the last tape we had in stock last week. I've put in another order, but I haven't received the shipment yet.

Josie: Oh, no. I can't postpone this presentation. It's taken me months to get the doctors at the hospital to agree to see it and weeks to find a date and time when they were all available.

Bob: Let me see what I can do. I'll get back to you right away. Where can I reach you?

Josie: I'm leaving to make some sales calls, so you can try reaching me in my car.

Bob: Your car phone number is in the rep listing. It hasn't changed, has it?

Josie: No, it hasn't.

Bob: I'll call you back as soon as I can.

Josie: Bye.
Bob: Bye.

(Bob calls Mike Ciliano, the marketing manager for Cardilon. Mike is at the headquarters building.)

Mike: Mike Ciliano.
Bob: Hi, Mike. It's Bob Donnelly in the southern regional office.
Mike: How are you doing?
Bob: Fine, thanks. Busy as usual.
Mike: What's up?
Bob: Josie Laker, the Atlanta rep, has an important video presentation of Cardilon planned for Thursday at Langston Memorial Hospital. She checked her copy of the video last night, and it's defective. We don't have any more copies on hand. Do you have one she can use?
Mike: Langston Memorial is a big account. Let me check to see what I have on my shelf. (pause) Bob, I have an extra copy. I'll send it to you express.
Bob: I think it would be best if you send it directly to Josie. Her address is on the rep listing.
Mike: Okay. I'll get it in the mail to her right away.
Bob: Thanks a lot.
Mike: No problem.
Bob: Good-bye.
Mike: Bye.

(Bob calls Josie on her car phone and tells her that a videocassette is being sent to her express.)

Bob must be as adept at making calls as he is at receiving them. Both these telephone activities can be handled with relative ease if professional procedures are followed.

Objectives

After completing this chapter, you should be able to:

- Answer the phone appropriately and professionally.

- Determine when it is appropriate to use voice mail, create a proper voice mail greeting, retrieve messages from voice mail, and leave complete voice mail messages.

- Take and leave complete and accurate phone messages.

- Apply the correct procedures for putting callers on hold and transferring calls.

- Handle difficult, unwanted, or confidential calls.

- Distinguish the different kinds of outgoing calls and when it is appropriate to use each.

- Determine when it is appropriate to send faxes and follow the correct procedures for sending them.

- Carefully plan your outgoing calls.

Receiving Calls

Workers often complain that they cannot get any work done because the phone doesn't stop ringing. It is sometimes difficult to remember that talking on the phone is work—speaking with customers, clients, coworkers, and suppliers can be as important as any other work done in an office.

In several respects, handling **incoming calls** is more difficult than making outgoing calls. For one thing, you never know when a call will come in. So despite whatever else you may be doing, you must answer the phone appropriately and not sound annoyed at the interruption. Incoming calls are also a challenge because you don't know what's coming. The call could be about a problem, complaint, or a difficult question that will take you some time to answer.

Answering the phone in jobs that focus on incoming calls, such as taking orders in a mail-order business, do not have the same element of uncertainty as do calls to people in other jobs. People who process orders are given specific guidelines to follow that provide structure to the incoming calls.

The more experience you gain at answering the phone, the easier it will be to handle anything that may come up.

ANSWERING THE PHONE

In an office, phones should be answered on the first ring whenever possible. What you say when you answer the phone will depend on the kind of telephone system your company has. If your company has a system in which an operator or

Fig. 4-1

Make sure that you answer the phone in a way that is clear and helpful to the customer.

Courtesy of Sprint VCC.

an automated system answers the phone first and routes the calls to individuals, it is not necessary to state your company's name when you answer the phone. However, if the calls come directly to you, you should state your company's name and then your own name when you answer the phone. This lets callers know that they have reached the company and person they intended to reach.

Many professionals answer the phone by stating only their name. For callers who know exactly whom they are calling and how this person will answer the phone, there is no problem in hearing just a person's name. But for callers who are calling without this knowledge, hearing someone's name as the phone is answered can often be confusing and difficult to make out. It is not uncommon for the caller to ask for the person by name despite the fact that the person receiving the call just stated his or her name.

USING VOICE MAIL

More and more companies are using voice mail systems. Voice mail has many advantages, but they must be understood to be used most effectively. Following are some guidelines for using voice mail:

Creating the Greeting. Some voice mail systems have a prerecorded greeting. With this kind of system, only your name is recorded in your voice. Other systems allow you to record your own personalized greeting. You should state your company name, if applicable, your name, and brief instructions for the caller.

Retrieving Messages. On most equipment a light on the phone will indicate that you have a voice message or messages. Before you listen to the messages, have paper and pen in hand so that you are prepared to write down names, phone numbers, and other important information that will come at you quickly. When leaving recorded messages, people often speak faster than they do when giving messages to a person, and they rarely repeat information. Also, there is no opportunity for feedback, so you may have to listen to the messages more than once to get all the information.

Deciding When to Use Voice Mail. Voice mail is ideally suited for taking messages when you are away from your telephone for a brief time. You may also elect to use voice mail when you are meeting with someone and do not want to interrupt your discussion to answer the phone. If you are working on something urgent or something that requires intense concentration, you may decide not to answer your phone for a while.

You should not use voice mail to answer your phone all the time. If callers reach a recording each time they call, they may become angry and frustrated.

If you are planning to be out of the office for several days, you should change your standard voice mail greeting to let callers know that you are unavailable. You should also provide the name and number of someone who can help them in your absence. If you cannot change the greeting, arrange to have someone check on your messages or call your system frequently to retrieve your messages. Most systems allow you to retrieve messages from outside phones. You may also be able to direct interoffice calls to the voice mail system and outside calls to someone, such as an assistant or receptionist, who can take a live message.

ARRANGING PHONE COVERAGE

Under no circumstances should a phone in an office ever go unanswered during normal business hours. If you do not have voice mail or some other telephone message system and you must leave your office for a few minutes, an hour, a day, or a week, always arrange **phone coverage;** that is, have someone answer your phone. This is especially important at lunchtime when most people are gone at the same time. At least one person should be available to answer calls.

TAKING MESSAGES

Offices usually have **telephone message forms,** which most employees keep near their phones. When you take a message for someone, use the form and be sure to fill in all parts. Remember to sign your name or initials.

If there are no forms available, make sure that your message includes the following information:

- Date

- Time

- Name of caller

- Company affiliation of caller, if any

- Caller's telephone number, including area code

- Message

- Your name or initials

Be sure to provide feedback when you take a message. Repeat all important information and ask questions if you are not sure of something that was said.

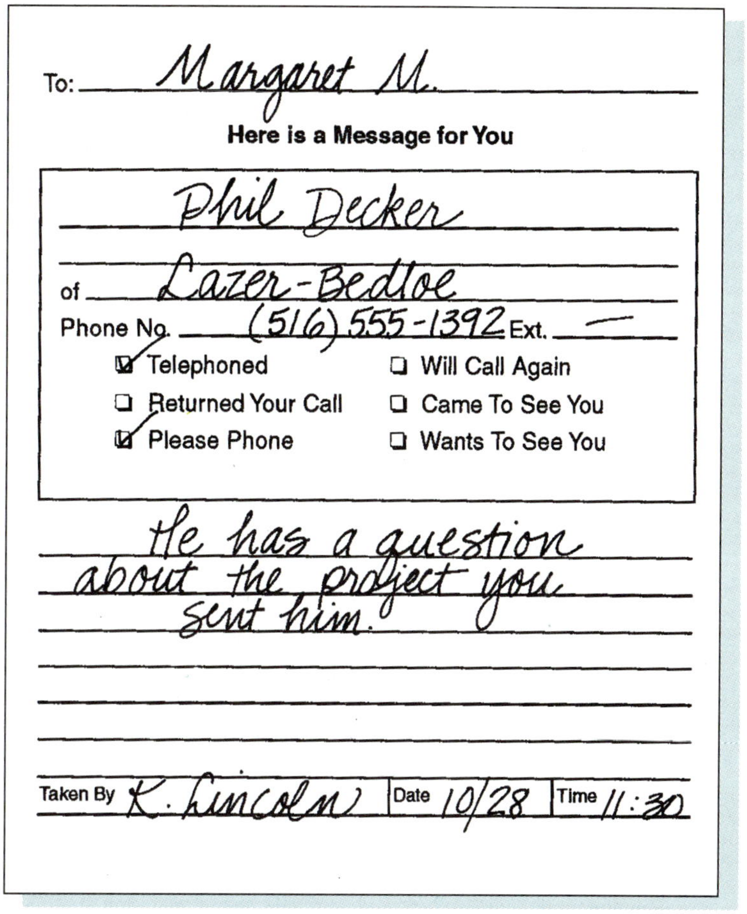

To: _Margaret M._

Here is a Message for You

Phil Decker

of _Lazer-Bedloe_

Phone No. _(516) 555-1392_ Ext. _—_

☑ Telephoned   ❏ Will Call Again
❏ Returned Your Call   ❏ Came To See You
☑ Please Phone   ❏ Wants To See You

He has a question about the project you sent him.

Taken By _K. Lincoln_   Date _10/28_   Time _11:30_

Figure 4-2

A completed telephone message form.

PUTTING CALLERS ON HOLD AND TRANSFERRING CALLS

When you start a job in a new company or when a new phone system is installed, learn how the system works and how you can handle routine functions such as putting a caller on hold or transferring calls.

Putting Callers on Hold

Follow basic telephone etiquette for putting a caller on hold:

- Do not put a caller on hold unless it is necessary.

- Never answer the phone and say "Hold on, please," before the caller has a chance to speak.

- Never just put the phone down on the desk instead of pushing the hold button.

- Always tell callers that they are being put on hold.

- Always check in with callers after about 30 seconds and at regular short intervals to let them know that you are aware that they are still on hold.

- If callers have been on hold for some time, ask if they want to continue to hold.

Transferring Calls

You may occasionally receive calls that must be transferred to someone else in your company. When this happens, make sure that the person you are transferring callers to is the person who can help them. Always provide callers with the name and number of the person they are being transferred to, so that they have recourse if the transfer doesn't go through or if the person they are being transferred to is not there.

Many people believe that it is preferable that you put the caller on hold and speak with the person the call is being transferred to before you put the call through. This allows the person receiving the transferred call to determine whether or not to take the call and also provides that person with the opportunity to greet the caller appropriately.

BEING PUT ON THE SPOT

Because so much of business is conducted in a hurry, letter writing has been at least partially replaced by telephone calls. One advantage of a letter over a phone call is that a letter gives the recipient time—to think, to gather information, to discuss issues, or to seek advice from others. You may be asked questions in a phone call that require time for you to formulate an answer. Do not let yourself be pushed into responding if you are not ready. You can assure the caller that you will respond by a certain date or time.

You may also be asked over the phone for an opinion or evaluation of something that you have not yet had time to look at. Rather than admit this, people are inclined to respond. So long as the response is noncommital, this is okay. Consider the following situation:

Frank: Frank Romano.

Doris: Hello, Frank. This is Doris Skinner. I'm calling to find out when we will have the signed contract so that we can start production on the new machine part for you.

Frank: Well, Doris. I've been looking over your proposal, and it's not really what we had in mind.

Doris: Last week you said it looked fine.

Frank: I hadn't examined it thoroughly last week. Now that I've had a chance to go over it carefully, I see that the overall plan just won't work with our equipment.

Doris: But, Frank, last week you said that everything was fine. We've spent many hours working out the specifications and planning the production process.

Frank: I'm sorry about the misunderstanding, Doris. Maybe we can work together on something else in the future.

Doris: There is no misunderstanding. You said our proposal was fine. Now you say it isn't. I'd like to speak with your boss. Would you please transfer me?

1. What should Frank have said to Doris when he spoke with her last week?

_____

_____

_____

2. Is Doris justified in being angry? Why or why not?

_____

_____

_____

3. Did Frank handle the rejection of the proposal appropriately? What, if anything, did he do right? What, if anything, did he do wrong?

_____

_____

_____

Suppose that you have looked at whatever the caller has sent you and you don't like it, it isn't very good, or it's not what you expected. It is certainly acceptable to tell the caller this over the phone. However, it may be easier, more tactful, and even kinder to state your objections in a letter, where you have time to choose your words carefully. If you prefer to do this, offer the caller noncommital responses and then follow up with a letter.

DEALING WITH UNWANTED CALLERS

Many people in business answer their own phones. Since no one is screening calls for them, they will occasionally receive calls that they would rather not receive. These calls may be from vendors, creditors, or others who want something or want to sell something.

Calls from Vendors

Calls from vendors are not always unwanted. Companies are often dependent upon good relationships with vendors to ensure good service and prompt delivery of needed products. Unsolicited calls from vendors should not necessarily be considered unwanted. Future circumstances may arise that would create a need for the vendor's product. However, there will be times when you do not want to or cannot spend the time to listen to a vendor's sales pitch. You should say so and ask the vendor to send you information that you can look at when you have time.

If you are certain that you will never have a need for the vendor's product, say so. There is no point in stringing someone along.

Calls from Creditors

If a person and/or company has done work, they have every reason to expect that they will be paid for it in a timely manner. Despite the fact that they are justified in calling to ask about their money, calls from creditors are often viewed as intrusive and annoying. However, the creditors are entitled to information about their payment. If you are in a position to provide the information, tell them when they can expect payment. If you work for a company with limited cash available and you know that you will not be able to pay the creditor for a certain amount of time, say so. In such circumstances, honesty is better than stalling or making up answers that are not true.

In large companies, people receive invoices and then route them for approval. The invoices ultimately end up in the accounting or accounts payable department. Checks are written and sent without the knowledge of the employee who received the invoice. In such situations, tell the creditor that you will contact accounting and find out when the payment will be made.

If you often receive invoices, it is a good idea to find out who in accounting can help you and develop a good relationship with that person.

HANDLING PROBLEM CALLS

In dealing with people who are unreasonable or overly emotional, never let yourself become defensive. Also, do not allow yourself to be drawn into an angry interchange. This is not to suggest that you will not become angry on occasion. So long as you behave appropriately and say the correct things in a normal tone of voice, there is nothing wrong with being angry. Take care in not allowing your emotions to control what you say or how you say it. You must remember to maintain your professional composure. For more on dealing with difficult callers, see Chapter 8.

■ Making Calls

Jobs often require that employees make **outgoing calls**. Frequently, they may call the same people inside or outside the company, thus establishing telephone relationships with people they may never meet. It should be noted that an excessive number of or overlong personal calls are not acceptable in a business office, and many companies consider this a serious problem.

There are a number of different types of business calls, and calls are made for a number of different reasons.

TYPES OF CALLS

Business telephone calls fall into three categories: interoffice, local, and long distance. There are factors that you should know about each.

Figure 4-3

Many jobs require that employees make telephone calls.

Courtesy of Sprint VCC.

Interoffice Calls

Unless you are calling the president of the company or some other high-level manager, you can assume that you can be more informal in making **interoffice calls** than in calls outside the company, especially if you know the people you are calling. However, regardless of the degree of informality, you still need to be clear in identifying yourself and in stating the reason for the call.

Often, employees in large companies do not know the people they are calling if they are calling outside their own department or division. These calls should be treated in the same way as calls to people outside the company would be.

Some large companies have branches or divisions scattered throughout the country, or they have large regional sales offices in key cities. In such cases, companies may arrange to have tie-lines connecting headquarters and other parts of the company. **Tie-lines** are special long-distance telephone connections that are less expensive to use than regular telephone lines. If your company has tie-lines to other parts of the country, be sure to use them when you call. This will save your company money.

Companies frequently have end-of-the-month telephone reports which list all the long-distance calls made from each telephone extension. These reports can be programmed to indicate when a tie-line was used and when a tie-line could have been used but was not. Managers review the reports for their departments and will be unhappy to see that employees are not using tie-lines and thus saving money for the department's telephone budget.

Local Calls

Dealing with local calls is fairly straightforward. Note that in some parts of the country, local calls may be made to different area codes. For example, New York City has two local area codes—212 and 718. Los Angeles also has two—213 and 818. Regional calls are calls within the area immediately surrounding the company. These calls are more expensive than local calls, but less expensive than long distance.

Most offices have local telephone directories (the white and yellow pages). You should find out where they are located and use them rather than call information, a call for which your company will be charged.

Long-Distance Calls

Long-distance calls may range from a call to the next county, to a call across the country, to a call to another country. (For information on international calls, see Chapter 6.) When you call someone in a state far from where you are, you need to determine what time it is in the distant location before you make the call.

The continental United States is divided into four time zones: Eastern, Central, Mountain, and Pacific. The time zone boundaries do not always follow state borders, so some states are in two time zones.

A time zone map, like the one shown in Figure 4-4, appears in your local telephone directory. In addition to time zone boundaries, the map also indicates area codes for major cities in each state, which can prove helpful when you need to find a phone number for another state or area code. To reach long-distance information, dial 1, then the area code, then 555-1212.

It is earliest in the east. For each time zone, subtract one hour as you move west and add one hour as you move east. For example, if it's one o'clock in Oregon (Pacific time zone), it's two o'clock in Montana (Mountain time zone), three o'clock in Iowa (Central time zone), and four o'clock in Maryland (Eastern time zone).

PACIFIC   MOUNTAIN   CENTRAL   EASTERN

Figure 4-4

Time-zone map.

When you make long-distance calls, you must plan so that you are calling at a time when people will be in their offices. You can assume that if you are in the Eastern time zone, you will make your calls to California in the afternoon, which will be morning in the west. And conversely, if you are in the west, you will have to make your calls east in the morning.

Long-distance calls fall into three categories: station-to-station, person-to-person, and collect.

Direct calls (sometimes referred to as station-to-station calls) are those that are made when you dial directly, without operator assistance.

Person-to-person calls are calls requiring operator assistance. You dial the operator, or 0, instead of 1, then the area code, then the number. When the operator or automated attendant comes on the line, you indicate that you want to make a person-to-person call. This means that you want to speak with a specific person and no one else. The operator will put through the call and ask for the person you wish to speak to. If the person is there, the call is connected and the operator hangs up. If the person is not there, the call is not connected and you are not charged for the call.

Person-to-person calls are more expensive than direct calls. However, if you weigh the fact that you may have to pay for a direct call even if the person you are calling is not there, the costs may balance out in the end.

Collect calls are calls for which the receiver rather than the sender must pay. Operator assistance is required. The operator will put through the call and ask the recipient of the call whether he or she will accept a collect call from the sender. If the recipient says yes, the call is connected; if no, it is not.

It is unlikely that you will make collect calls from your own office. Sometimes, people who travel for business call the home office collect when they are on the road. If you find that you will be traveling and you want to call the office collect rather than charge the call to your hotel bill, let whomever you will be calling know ahead of time that you are planning to do this so that the collect call will be accepted.

Credit Card Calls

Workers who do a lot of business travel find telephone credit cards very helpful. The caller keys in the credit card account number, and the call is automatically charged to the account. Credit card calls can be made easily from any phone. Some phones are specially designed to accept credit cards, so the caller does not have to key in the account number. The caller slides the card through a slot that reads the number off the magnetic tape on the card. These special phones are frequently found in airports, train stations, and bus depots.

411

Some telephone credit cards are now linked to a voice recognition and response system. Cardholders provide the long-distance carrier with their own voice saying key phrases such as "Call home," "Call office," or "Call Fred," and the telephone number for each. The system is then programmed to accept only the voice of the cardholder. It can distinguish the commands given orally and will automatically dial the correct number. Not only does this simplify calling, but it also prevents unauthorized people from using the credit card number.

Figure 4-5

Telephone credit cards are easily used with a Touch Tone™ phone.

SENDING FAXES

Faxes have made it possible for people to conduct business around the world with great speed. It is possible to send pages of detailed information, drawings, plans, and so forth in minutes where previously it may have taken a day (with express mail delivery service) or more.

Most companies have fax machines set up on different lines from those that receive telephone calls. In order to send a fax, you must have the fax number of the person who is to receive the fax. Many business cards indicate the telephone number and the fax number.

Rarely do individuals have their own fax machines. Fax machines are commonly designated for a department, division, or floor. For this reason, the sender must indicate on the materials being sent whom the fax is intended for. Often

Figure 4-6a

A fax cover sheet.

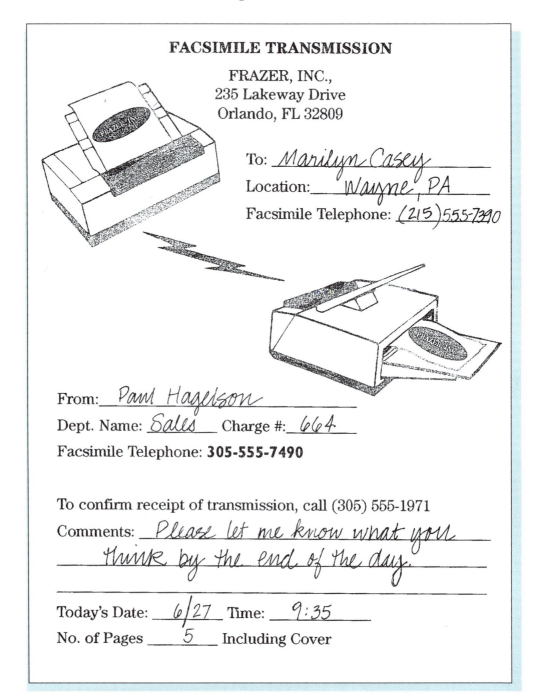

FACSIMILE TRANSMISSION

FRAZER, INC.,
235 Lakeway Drive
Orlando, FL 32809

To: *Marilyn Casey*
Location: *Wayne, PA*
Facsimile Telephone: *(215) 555-7390*

From: *Paul Hagelson*
Dept. Name: *Sales* Charge #: *664*
Facsimile Telephone: **305-555-7490**

To confirm receipt of transmission, call (305) 555-1971
Comments: *Please let me know what you think by the end of the day.*

Today's Date: *6/27* Time: *9:35*
No. of Pages *5* Including Cover

Figure 4-6b

Paste-on form for

faxes.

FAX		No. of pages *4*
To *M. Casey*		From *Paul Hagleson*
Co. *Frazer*		Co. *Frazer*
Dept. *Production*		Phone# *(305) 555-9373*
Fax# *(215) 555-7390*		Fax# *(305) 555-7490*

companies have cover sheets that must be filled out by the sender. The cover sheet asks for such information as name, department, and the number of pages being sent. Since each page that is sent costs extra, some companies have a paper strip requiring the same fill-in information. This strip is pasted across the top of the first page of the fax.

Because faxes are quick and easy to send and because they are in widespread business use, people are inclined to send faxes in situations that do not warrant the speed or expense. (The cost of sending a fax is the equivalent of a long-distance call.) After all, everything is not an emergency. Employees should consider whether something must be received immediately or whether first-class mail will be acceptable. (Note that overnight mail delivery can be more expensive than a fax, depending on what is being sent.)

Planning Calls

You can safely assume that every business call has a purpose, or objective. The objective may be something very simple, like answering a question or returning a call without knowing the reason for the call. Some objectives may be more complicated. They may involve making or confirming travel or meeting plans, doing research for a report, or finalizing a deal or sale.

Every call you make will require some preparation and/or planning, however minimal. At the very least, you should have a pen and paper ready so that you can take notes. If you are responding to a letter or memo, have it in front of you. If there's a possibility that other relevant documents will be discussed, have the file handy.

Complicated or very important calls should be planned carefully. It is a good idea to list key points you want to cover or questions you want to ask. This way you will be less likely to forget something vital as you get caught up in the flow of the conversation.

In planning a call, you should first ask yourself, "What do I want to accomplish or achieve from this call?" Then work backwards in listing the steps that will be necessary to reach the objective.

Suppose, for example, that you have been involved in negotiating a lease for warehouse facilities. The negotiations are almost complete, but there are a few loose ends that must be tied up before the lease can be signed. In this situation, your objective is to finalize the terms of the lease. You should list the issues that remain unresolved or the questions that are unanswered. You may also list "what if" questions, which will be dependent on answers to other questions you ask. You may want to confirm the issues that have been resolved previously so that there are no misunderstandings. If this is the case, make a list of the resolved issues as well. Once the call is completed for something as complex and important as a legal negotiation, it is a good idea to follow up with a letter summarizing what was agreed to.

This kind of thorough planning and preparation will make your phone transactions manageable and will enhance your professional image inside and outside the company.

LEAVING MESSAGES

When making business calls, you will frequently be unable to reach the person you are calling. In such cases, you will have to leave a message. If someone answers the phone for the person you are calling, you will probably be asked for your name, number, company or department affiliation, and the reason for your call. If you are in a different time zone from the person you are calling, mention your location as part of the message since the person may not be able to tell your location from your area code alone.

If you reach someone's voice mail, you will have to provide the key information without being prompted. With voice mail, you must speak more slowly than you would when speaking to a person. An ideal message to leave on voice mail should include:

- Your name

- Your company or department affiliation

- Your phone number, including area code

- The time you are making the call

- Your location, if you are in a different time zone from the person you are calling

- A brief message

- A time when you will be available for a return call

Always repeat your name. Spell it out if the person you are calling does not know you. When you spell information over the phone, be especially careful to enunciate clearly. Certain letters sound alike over the phone. Use examples to clarify which letter you mean. For example:

B as in boy; P as in Peter
D as in David; T as in Tom
F as in Frank; S as in Susan
M as in Mary; N as in Nancy

Be sure to clarify whether you have said a five or a nine. And always repeat your phone number.

Maintaining Confidentiality

Certain types of phone calls require privacy. Calls concerning personnel matters, such as hiring, firing, promotions, demotions, layoffs, disciplinary matters, payroll matters (such as raises or salaries), and confidential company matters (such as sales, acquisitions, and mergers), should be made or taken behind closed doors or when few people are around.

If you work for someone who frequently deals in confidential matters, you must also respect that confidentiality. When leaving a phone message containing confidential information, fold the message form over and staple it, or put it in a sealed envelope.

Chapter Summary

- Receiving calls is more challenging than making calls because you never know when the phone will ring or what will confront you when you answer.

- Answer your phone so that it is clear to callers that they have reached the right company and the right person.

- Voice mail is helpful when you are out of your office or do not wish to be disturbed; voice mail should not be used to answer all calls all the time.

- Office phones must never go unanswered. Arrange phone coverage regardless of whether you will be out of the office for a few minutes or a few days.

- Most offices have telephone message forms. Messages should include the time and date of the call; the caller's name, phone number, and company affiliation; the message; and the name of the person who takes the message.

- Always tell callers that you are putting them on hold; always check in with callers to let them know that you are aware that they are still on hold; ask callers who have been on hold for a while whether they want to continue to wait.

- When transferring calls, provide the callers with the name and number of the person they are being transferred to.

- Do not allow yourself to be put on the spot by unexpected requests or questions or by being asked for a response you are not prepared to make. Answer noncommittally until you are in a position to respond appropriately.

- Although calls from vendors may be viewed as unwanted, they should be given careful consideration since good relationships with vendors are an important element in a company's success. However, if a vendor is selling something that you are sure you will never need, be honest and say so.

- Although calls from creditors may be annoying, people are entitled to receive the money they are owed. Do your best to let creditors know when they can expect to be paid.

- Three types of business calls are interoffice, local, and long distance.

- Interoffice calls may be more informal than calls to people outside the company. Tie-lines should be used when long-distance calls are made to other parts of the company.

- The continental United States is divided into four time zones: Eastern, Central, Mountain, and Pacific.

- The three kinds of long-distance calls are direct, person-to-person, and collect.

- Telephone credit cards are a convenience used by many people who travel for business. The account number is keyed into the phone, and the call is automatically charged to the account.

- Faxes require the use of a cover sheet or paste-on strip that identifies key information about the caller and the person being called.

- Effective business calls require careful planning and preparation. The objective of the call should be identified and then steps listed that will lead to achieving the objective.

- Confidential calls should be handled behind closed doors.

Key Terms

collect calls
credit card calls
direct calls
fax cover sheet
incoming calls
interoffice calls
outgoing calls
person-to-person calls
phone coverage
telephone message form
tie-line
time zone

Chapter Review

Write your answers to the questions that follow and be prepared to discuss them in class.

1. **State two reasons why it is more difficult to receive calls than to make them.**

    _____

    _____

    _____

    _____

    _____

2. **You work for a company in Portland, Oregon. You return to your office at 4:30 p.m. after a long meeting and listen to the messages on your voice mail. Among the messages is one from an important client in Florida asking for some information on a project you are working on for her. She needs the information as quickly as possible. You have the information available. How will you get the information to her? List your options.**

    _____

    _____

    _____

    _____

    _____

3. **You work in the shipping department of Langlan Manufacturing Company. Langlan has an automated central switchboard that answers the phone and routes calls by extension numbers being keyed in on Touch-Tone™ phones. How should you answer your own phone? Include as many ways as may be appropriate.**

    _____

    _____

    _____

    _____

    _____

4. **You are on the phone with the personnel manager of your company discussing a disciplinary problem concerning one of your workers. Someone comes into your office while you are on the phone and waits to speak with you while you are talking. What should you do? How might you have prevented this from happening?**

_____

_____

_____

_____

_____

5. **You receive a call from someone who asks for you by your first name only. This person says that he received a message from you on his voice mail, and he could not make out your last name. What should you have done when leaving the message that would have kept this from happening?**

_____

_____

_____

_____

_____

_____

<table>
<tr><td>**Audio Dialogue 4-1**</td><td>Read the background information below. Then turn on your audiocassette player and listen to Audio Dialogue 4-1. Turn off the player when the end of the dialogue is announced. NOTE: This dialogue is in two parts. Do not turn off the player after the first part. (Do not rewind the cassette.) Then answer the questions on the following pages.</td></tr>
</table>

Background: Lorraine Irving is an editorial assistant in the high school academic book division of World Communications, Inc., a large publishing company. Her job is a mix of editorial and secretarial responsibilities. She was an administrative assistant for eight years before she earned her bachelor's degree and decided to try editorial work, so she has many years of business experience although she is a relatively new employee with World. She often answers the phone for several editors who travel a great deal.

1. Lorraine spent a lot of time resolving Mr. Morgan's problem even though it was not directly related to her own department or work. Do you think that she handled the situation appropriately? If yes, explain why. If no, how else might she have handled the situation?

_____

_____

_____

_____

_____

2. Mr. Morgan is not the first or only person to be transferred around a company. This situation is not uncommon in very large, diverse companies. What do you think large companies should do to avoid this kind of problem?

_____

_____

_____

_____

_____

3. In Chapter 3, you learned about feedback. Did both Lorraine and Mr. Morgan provide sufficient feedback to make their communication successful? Explain your answer; provide examples.

_____

_____

_____

_____

_____

4. Do you think that Lorraine's previous work experience helped her to handle the situation? Explain why or why not.

_____

_____

_____

_____

PROFESSIONAL TELEPHONE MANAGEMENT

Chapter

5

On the Job: Finding Information and Handling Travel Plans

Eliot Freeman is assistant director of research for a company that develops and manufactures medical pet supplies. In a conversation with a colleague, he learns about breakthrough research being conducted at a veterinary college. He is interested in learning more about the work being conducted and asks his colleague for information so that he can contact the doctors doing the research. All that his colleague knows is the name of the college. With this small bit of information, Eliot will be able to call the doctors.

He knows the location of the college, so he checks the telephone directory for the area code and then calls long-distance information for the number. Once he gets the number, he calls the college switchboard and asks for the research department. He explains his situation to the person who answers the phone. That person gives him the name of one of the veterinarians involved in the research and tells Eliot that the doctor in charge will be in his office at 3 o'clock in the afternoon.

Eliot calls back and speaks with the doctor, who invites him to visit the college and see firsthand the work that is being done. Eliot accepts the invitation and then calls a travel agent who books his flight and his hotel room.

A week later, Eliot is at the college and is given the opportunity to see the exciting research, which may have an impact on his own business.

People in all lines of work—managers, professionals, support staff, and all others—conduct numerous transactions by phone. The telephone is used for conducting research, making travel plans, arranging meetings and conferences, scheduling appointments, and so on. For the most part, the procedures to be followed in conducting business over the phone are the same for all workers. There are some additional issues that relate to support staff alone.

Objectives

After completing this chapter, you should be able to:

- Handle administrative phone procedures such as screening calls, taking messages, taking the initiative, and keeping telephone records.

- Conduct research over the phone.

- Make arrangements over the phone, including scheduling meetings and appointments and making travel and hotel reservations.

- Place orders by phone.

- Arrange and conduct a teleconference.

Handling Administrative Procedures

Although many managers and professionals answer their own telephones, some still have their assistants answer the telephone for them. And despite voice mail, assistants may be asked to answer the telephone for their managers if the manager is out of the office.

ANSWERING FOR THE MANAGER

If you are an assistant, you need to find out how your manager would like you to handle his or her telephone. If your manager expects you to answer the phone for him or her on a regular basis, this should be clear from the outset. You should also find out whether your manager has a preference for what you say when you answer. If the manager does not state a preference, it is customary to say, "Mr. Miller's office," or "Margaret Hailey's office."

As mentioned in an earlier chapter, if there is no central switchboard, the person answering the phone should state the company name as well as the name of the person being called; for example, "Bitterman and Boggs, Margaret Hailey's office."

Even if managers normally answer their own telephones, there will be times when you may be expected to answer the phone for them. These may include when managers are meeting with someone in their office or when they are working on something urgent and cannot be disturbed. You may also be expected to answer if they are out of the office for a few minutes or several days. This may be the case even if your manager has voice mail.

Screening Calls

If an assistant answers the phone for the manager all the time, the assistant should **screen calls,** which includes finding out whether there are certain callers or types of calls (such as sales calls) that the manager does not wish to have put through. Sometimes managers may not wish to speak with someone for just a day or so, perhaps while the manager is getting an answer to a question, formulating a decision, or reviewing materials submitted by the caller.

Calls such as these should be handled with courtesy and tact. You can say that the manager is in a meeting, out of the office, or simply cannot come to the phone. Never promise a return call. You can, however, promise that you will give the manager the message.

Taking Messages

Follow the guidelines provided in Chapter 4 for taking telephone messages. As an assistant, you should review the message to see whether you can do something to make things easier for the manager. For example, if someone calls as a follow-up to a letter sent to the manager, attach the letter to the message when you present it to the manager.

Taking the Initiative

Once an assistant has been on the job for a while, certain callers and certain situations will become familiar. There may be instances in which the assistant can handle the matter alone. If this occurs, give the manager a message about the call and the action taken if, in your judgement, the manager needs to be informed.

Figure 5-1

An assistant should ask who the caller is before giving the call to the manager.

Photo by Alan Brown/Photonics.

Handling Special Situations

Even though managers may be in a meeting or ask not to be disturbed, assistants must use their judgment in screening calls to determine whether to interrupt a meeting or the manager's urgent work. You can usually ascertain the importance or urgency of the situation from the tone of the caller or who the caller is.

If the manager is in a meeting, write a note explaining who is on the phone and the critical nature of the call. Knock on the door of the meeting and quietly enter and hand the manager the note. Wait to see whether he or she will leave the meeting to take the call.

Read the background information below. Then turn on your audiocassette player and listen to Audio Dialogue 5-1. Turn off the player when the end of the dialogue is announced. (Do not rewind the cassette.) Then answer the questions below.

Background: Li Chan has worked at Alisson Ray Fashion Company as assistant to Yvette Malraux for almost a year. Yvette, production manager for the women's hat design and manufacturing company, usually answers her own phone. She has asked Li to answer her phone whenever she is out of the office—either at in-house meetings or away on business. Today, Yvette is in an all-day meeting.

Audio Dialogue 5-1

1. If Li were not familiar with Yvette's work, how might the situation have ended differently?

_____

_____

_____

2. If this situation arose before faxes existed, how might the error have caused a problem?

_____

_____

_____

3. Do you think that Li should have replaced one bid with the other? Why or why not?

_____

_____

_____

KEEPING TELEPHONE RECORDS

Some managers and some specific types of businesses, such as law offices, keep records of all incoming and, possibly, all outgoing calls. These records are usually called a telephone log. They may be preprinted forms, carbon copy forms, forms made up in the office, or computerized. Whichever is the case, you must develop the habit of recording all calls without fail.

A **telephone log** usually requires the following information:

■ Date

■ Time

- Name and affiliation of caller (for incoming calls)
- Name and affiliation of person being called (for outgoing calls)
- Purpose of call
- Action taken, if any or if known

Figure 5-2

A telephone log.

TELEPHONE LOG

Date	Time	Caller/Co.	Purpose	Action Taken

Conducting Telephone Research

All workers, regardless of level or title, must obtain information over the phone on occasion. The information may be as simple as a telephone number in another city or as complex as statistical data for a report. The telephone provides access to huge amounts of diverse information.

USING TELEPHONE DIRECTORIES

The white and yellow pages contain more information than names, addresses, and telephone numbers. Depending on the size of the city you are in, the white and yellow pages may be in one or two volumes. The front part of each directory may contain the following information:

- Emergency numbers, such as police, fire, and ambulance

- Community service numbers, such as consumer problems, education, family and children's services, health care, poison control, street maintenance, suicide prevention, and so on

- Directory assistance information—numbers for local, regional, long-distance, and 800 numbers

- Information on how to make operator-assisted calls.

- A time zone map of the United States and parts of Canada, including area codes for key cities

- A list of area codes for many U.S. and some Canadian cities

- A list of international country and city calling codes

- A list of two-letter state abbreviations

In addition, local telephone directories also contain a section of **blue pages,** which lists numbers for local, state, and federal agencies.

If you must conduct research over the telephone, directories are a good place to start since they may provide you with information that may help you obtain other information.

Figure 5-3

If you must do research over the phone, the telephone directory is a good place to start.

LOCATING PEOPLE

Occasions will arise in which you need to call someone for whom you do not have a number. For example, you need to call an individual for whom you have a name and address but no telephone number. Or you need to call someone who works for a company. You have the person's name and the company name but no number.

As long as you have someone's name and the name of the city in which he or she lives (a partial address, such as "on 23rd Street," is also helpful), you should be able to obtain the phone number. If the person whose number you are looking for lives in the same city as you, simply check the local telephone directory.

If the person you need to reach lives in another city, you can find the number by calling long-distance information. The number is 1-area code-555-1212. If you do not know the area code of the city you need to call, you can check the list of area codes for U.S. cities in the telephone directory. If the one you need is not listed, you can call local information (411) to get the area code and then dial long-distance information.

If you need to reach someone at work and do not have the number of the company, you can obtain it the same way you obtain the number of an individual. Even companies in which everyone has a direct-dial number have central numbers for the general public. Once you reach the general number, you will be switched to the person you want to reach. Make a note of the person's extension.

LOCATING INFORMATION

Locating information by phone requires preparation, persistence, and patience. In order to obtain the information you need, you must find the right place (source), the right phone number, and the right person.

Preparation

As mentioned in Chapter 4, when you make business calls, you should make notes of key points you wish to cover before you make the call. This is especially important in conducting research over the phone. If you have a great deal of ground to cover, you may consider writing one or two questions per page in a notepad, leaving the rest of the page for notes.

Patience

You may recall the problem Lyle Morgan had in the audio dialogue in Chapter 4. He was transferred from one person to another in a large publishing company. If you do not have the specific name of a person or department, this could easily happen to you. Although it is unlikely that you can prevent this from happening entirely, you may be able to limit your frustration by giving the first person you speak with (often a company telephone operator) as much information as possible so that he or she will be able to connect you with the right division or department. For example, if Mr. Morgan had mentioned the title and author of the book, he might have had better luck.

Persistence

Depending on the complexity of the information you require, you may not be able to locate the correct source immediately. You will have to be persistent and creative in locating the organization that has the information you need. If the information you need is specific to the business you are in and the customers or other businesses you deal with, your task is relatively simple. However, you may not know the source or you may know the name of the company to contact but not know where it is located.

If you do not know where to find information you need, the first place to start may be by asking coworkers for suggestions. You may also call your local public library. Even if the librarian cannot provide you with the information you need, he or she may be able to suggest a starting point. The library is also a good source for finding the location of a company. Once you know what city it is in, you can call information and get the phone number. Another way to find out where a company is located is by looking at products it produces or published ads. Note: Not all public libraries provide information over the phone.

Making Arrangements over the Phone

The telephone makes it possible for workers to make arrangements for all kinds of services and events without ever leaving the office.

SCHEDULING MEETINGS AND APPOINTMENTS

When you have to set up a meeting, always have a preferred date and time. Also consider alternate dates and/or times in case people who must attend the meeting are not available for your first choice. Make a list of the people who will be asked to attend the meeting and note those who must attend versus those who do not have to attend. Do not reserve a meeting or conference room until the date and time are confirmed. However, you should check on the availability of conference rooms so that you will not arrange your meeting at a time when none is available.

When you start calling the intended participants, you may not reach the person you are calling directly. If you reach an assistant, he or she can check the manager's calendar and let you know whether the manager is available. If you reach voice mail, leave all the information—date, time, and purpose of the meeting—in your message. In both cases, be sure to request a callback to confirm that the messages have been received and that all the participants are available.

Once this is confirmed, you should do two things: reserve a conference room if one is necessary and contact all participants to confirm the meeting and to provide necessary details, such as date, time, purpose, and location. The contact may be through memo or by phone.

Following is an illustration of what it's like to set up a meeting. Barbara Ohlmeyer is setting up a meeting to discuss approval of a new project.

Eileen:	Janet Parker's office.
Barbara:	Hi, Eileen. It's Barbara Ohlmeyer. Is Janet in?
Eileen:	No, she's out of the office today. Can I help you?
Barbara:	I'm setting up a meeting to discuss approval of the Graham-Grant project. I'd like to arrange the meeting for next Thursday, May 10, at 10 o'clock. Do you know if Janet is available then?
Eileen:	Let me check her calendar. Hold on just a moment.
Barbara:	Okay.
Eileen:	Janet is available then. I'll pencil you in for Thursday the tenth at 10 a.m.
Barbara:	Good. I'll get back to you to confirm.
Eileen:	Thanks.
Barbara:	Good-bye.
Eileen:	Bye.

Jason:	Jason Tanner.
Barbara:	Hello, Jason. It's Barbara Ohlmeyer.
Jason:	What can I do for you, Barbara?
Barbara:	I'm setting up a meeting to get approval for the Graham-Grant project.
Jason:	Oh, I'm glad to hear that that project is ready to begin.
Barbara:	So am I. It's involved a lot of my time. I'd like to hold the meeting next Thursday, the tenth, at 10 o'clock.
Jason:	Uh oh. I'm going to be out of the office from Wednesday to Friday of next week. Do you think you can hold the meeting on Tuesday?
Barbara:	I should have all the papers ready by then. What time would be good for you?
Jason:	I'd prefer the morning.
Barbara:	How about ten?
Jason:	That will be fine.
Barbara:	That's next Tuesday, the eighth, at 10 a.m.
Jason:	Right.
Barbara:	I'll get back to you to confirm and let you know where the meeting will be.
Jason:	OK. Thanks.
Barbara:	Bye.
Jason:	Bye.

1. Barbara has to contact Janet to let her know about the change in the meeting date and find out whether Janet is available for the rescheduled meeting. Barbara also has four more people to contact about the meeting. Should she

call Janet's office immediately, or should she wait until she has made the other calls? Explain your answer.

_____

_____

_____

2. If Barbara was the manager of all the people who are supposed to attend the meeting, do you think she would go about setting up the meeting in the same way? Explain.

_____

_____

_____

_____

From the example, you can see that setting up a meeting can be time-consuming and occasionally frustrating.

MAKING RESERVATIONS

If some meeting participants are from out of town or if you are an out-of-town participant at a meeting, hotel arrangements and travel plans will have to be made. If you are handling the meeting, you may also have to consider lunch and dinner arrangements. Of course, you may have to make hotel or travel arrangements for others even if you are not attending the meeting.

Arranging Air Travel

There are several ways that flight reservations can be handled. You can use your company's travel department, if it has one. You can use a travel agent (many companies have arrangements with outside agents), or you can contact the airlines directly. Regardless of whom you contact, you will need to provide specific information concerning your own preferences or those of the person you are making the reservations for. These include:

- Departure and arrival times. If you are making the reservations for someone else, ask for alternate times in case flights at the preferred times are booked or do not exist

- Preferred airline (some travelers have preferences or may be accumulating frequent flyer miles)

- Airport preferences (some large cities have more than one)

- Seating preferences (window or aisle)

- Dietary restrictions, if any, for in-flight meals

- Preferred class of travel—first class, business class, or economy class. Many companies have restrictions against their employees flying first class, so you will need to know this

If you are making the reservations through a company travel department, you will need a **charge number** (so that the cost of the ticket can be charged against the department's travel budget) or a credit card number (including expiration date) against which the tickets can be charged. If the arrangements are made through a travel agent or airline, the credit card is all that will be necessary.

If you wish to arrange air travel through an airline, you can call the number listed in your local telephone directory or an 800 number. To reach information for 800 numbers, dial 1-800-555-1212.

When talking with the reservations clerk or travel agent, be sure to find out whether the traveler must change planes and whether there are stopovers on the flight. Also find out the price of the flight and whether there are any less expensive fares available. Depending on the days on which the trip is made, it may be possible to greatly decrease the price of the flight by staying an extra day. Of course, this should be weighed against the additional cost of hotel, meals, and other expenses.

Some travelers change their flight arrangements while they are traveling. You must find out whether the fare is nonrefundable, since this could have a serious impact on the traveler's plans.

Handling Hotel Reservations

To make hotel reservations, you can contact your company travel department, a travel agent, or the hotel directly. Most large hotel chains have 800 numbers you can call to make reservations at locations in the United States and overseas. It is a good idea to make travel arrangements before a hotel room is reserved because arrival times may affect hotel reservations. Find out if your company has any special discount arrangements with certain hotel chains.

As with air travel reservations, you should be prepared to answer a number of questions concerning your own preferences or those of the person you are making the reservations for.

Figure 5-4

You can make all kinds of business arrangements on the phone.

- Hotel preferences (specific hotel chain; older versus modern accommodations)

- High or low floor (some people do not like rooms on high floors; others prefer them)

- Smoking or nonsmoking floor (some hotels restrict smoking to certain floors for example, smoking may be permitted in rooms on the fourth, sixth, and eighth floors of a hotel)

- Location (there may be a convention center or company the traveler would like to be near)

- Room with a view (these are generally more expensive than those without a view)

- Meals (hotels in the United States usually do not include meals as part of the arrangement; hotels in Europe may or may not)

If you make hotel reservations over the phone, you should request written confirmation or a confirmation number from the travel department, travel agent, or hotel. Even if a traveler is scheduled to arrive in town early, it is a good idea to arrange that the reservation be held for a late arrival. This way, if the traveler is delayed, the room reservation will not be lost.

Placing Orders

Usually, ordering goods or services in business is done via purchase orders or other preprinted forms. However, there may be occasions when you find it necessary to order something by phone. When this occurs, plan the call carefully to ensure that you have all the information at hand that you will need to place the order.

If an order form or purchase order is available, use one as a model to see what kind of information is needed. It is a good idea to fill out the form even if you are not planning to send it. In this way, you will be sure to have all the information you need, and you will have your filled-out version of the form as a record of the order.

Often-requested information for orders includes:

- Item, stock, or product numbers

- Color

- Size

- Quantity

- Billing information, including a "bill to" name and address; some companies have "charge to" numbers that are used for purchases

- Shipping information, including the "ship to" address and whether any special handling is desired, such as express delivery

After something has been ordered by phone, you may wish to send a printed version of the order for confirmation.

Handling Teleconferences

Teleconferences may be held with audio equipment alone (conference calls) or may also include video equipment; computers may also be involved. Video teleconferences tend to be more formal than conference calls. A video teleconference cannot be held if the company does not have the appropriate teleconferencing equipment. Often a technician is on staff to handle the cameras and other technical equipment.

Video teleconferences are arranged much as a meeting would be, since all the participants must be at the location of the teleconference equipment at a specific time. Conference calls require some special planning and preparation. They also require that some simple procedures be followed to ensure success. Note that many of the procedures for a conference call are also applicable to calls involving speakerphones in which a number of people are participating in one call.

Some office telephone systems allow the user to arrange for a conference call without involving an outside operator. Review the user manual that comes with your telephone equipment before you begin to set up the call. If your phone system requires outside assistance, call the phone company's conference operator to ask for information before you begin making arrangements.

ARRANGING THE CALL

Regardless of whether you need the assistance of a conference operator, you must contact each participant ahead of time to establish a specific date and time for the call. It is important to stress that the time established for the call must be adhered to and that participants can expect to begin the conference within five to ten minutes of the scheduled time.

Each participant should be aware of who the other participants will be. Participants should also have an agenda (formal or informal) so that they can prepare for the conference.

At the appointed time, each participant will be contacted, either by you or the operator. Participants may also be given a telephone number to dial, which connects them to a "meet me" bridge.

DURING THE CALL

Once all participants are on the line, each should state his or her name. As the person who initiated the conference call, you will most likely function as the leader or facilitator.

The more people who are on the line, the more difficult it will be to know who is speaking. It will also be difficult to follow the conversation. Encourage participants to identify themselves when they begin speaking. Also request that they speak slowly. Discourage interruptions and two people talking at once.

If you are not able to, distribute a written agenda to each participant, at the least have one for yourself. A written agenda should help you keep people on track. Make sure that all important points are covered and resolved before the call is terminated.

Because conference calls can be confusing for participants to follow, it is a good idea to send a written summary of the call to everyone involved.

Chapter Summary

- An assistant may be expected to answer and screen calls for the manager as well as take messages and use some initiative in responding to callers.

- Some companies require that records be kept of all calls received or made; a telephone log is the form used to record incoming and outgoing calls.

- Local telephone directories are a helpful resource for conducting research over the phone.

- Planning, preparation, and patience are essential to gathering information by phone.

- When scheduling a meeting by phone, select the date and time of the meeting before contacting the participants; always confirm meeting arrangements.

- Air travel and hotel reservations may be arranged through your company's travel department, a travel agency, or the airline or hotel directly.

- When making flight reservations (your own or someone else's), know the following preferences of the traveler: departure and arrival times, airports, airlines, seating, dietary restrictions, and class of travel.

- When making hotel reservations (your own or someone else's), know the following preferences of the traveler: hotel, high or low floor, smoking or non-smoking floor, location, room with a view, and meals.

- Often-requested information for phone orders includes: item, stock, or product numbers; color; size; billing information; and shipping information.

- Participants in a conference call should speak slowly and clearly. They should state who they are when they are speaking and not speak when someone else is.

- The person who arranges a conference call functions as the leader; arranges the date and time of the call; prepares, distributes, and follows an agenda; and provides participants with written follow-up of the results of the conversation.

Key Terms

blue pages
charge number
on-line computer information service
screening calls
telephone log

Chapter Review

Write your answers to the questions that follow and be prepared to discuss them in class.

1. **You work for a company in Minnesota and are planning a business trip to Boston. Your company has discount arrangements with Marriott hotels. List three ways that you can make reservations at a Marriott hotel in Boston.**

2. **You are putting the finishing touches on a report that covers current market conditions for your product line. You need some additional information. You know the name of the company that has the information you need, and you know where the company is located. Explain how you will go about getting the information.**

3. **You have been asked to phone in an order for some office supplies for your department. You are given a list of supplies needed and the office supplies catalog. What should you do to ensure that the order you place is accurate and complete? Do you have all the information you need to place the order? If not, what additional information do you need?**

4. You are making hotel reservations for someone who will be meeting with members of your company. List two questions that you should ask this person before you make the hotel reservation.

5. You are assistant to Katharine Moran. She is in an important meeting with company executives. She receives a call from her husband who says that he must speak with her about an urgent personal matter. What should you do?

Read the background information below. Then turn on your audiocassette player and listen to Audio Dialogue 5-2. Turn off the player when the end of the dialogue is announced. (Do not rewind the cassette.) Then answer the questions on the following page.

Background: Charlotte Wyman is convention coordinator for a division of KyRee, a large sporting goods company. As convention coordinator, Charlotte handles arrangements for her division at all sporting goods conventions in North America, including the setup of the division's exhibits, dinner or party arrangements, and her division's entertainment suite. The job involves dozens of details from menus to floral arrangements to refreshments.

Jamal Peterson is assistant convention manager at the Rupert Hotel. Jamal handles hundreds of details as he works with people like Charlotte from different companies around the country. Charlotte must obtain preliminary information for a luncheon-fashion show planned for key retail buyers. She is on the phone with Jamal.

1. If Jamal had not offered to send Charlotte information about local models, how might Charlotte have gotten the information even though her company is more than a thousand miles away?

_____

_____

_____

_____

_____

2. Do you think that Charlotte will be able to arrange for the special flower colors by phone? If yes, explain. If no, how might this be handled?

_____

_____

_____

_____

_____

3. Both Charlotte and Jamal are professionals at handling conference arrangements. Sometimes companies have someone take care of conferences as a one-time job. Considering that the person making all the arrangements may not get to see the facilities before the conference, how might you go about handling a conference?

_____

_____

_____

_____

_____

INTERNATIONAL TELEPHONE COMMUNICATIONS

On the Job: Communicating in the Global Village

Lynette Peters works in the New Jersey office of TeleCom International. Her boss, Donald Iverson, left yesterday on a business trip to Moscow, Russia. As a consultant on satellite communications technology, he will be spending two weeks traveling abroad to assist various client companies. Lynette needs to contact Mr. Iverson to let him know of a change in his itinerary that was faxed to the office from a client he will be visiting in a few days. She decides to try to catch Mr. Iverson at his last appointment of the day. At 8 a.m. in New Jersey Lynette places a call to Moscow, knowing Mr. Iverson's appointment at a Moscow TV station is scheduled for 4 p.m. Moscow time. She reaches the station operator and asks to be connected to Mr. Buracek's office.

Buracek's secretary:	Hello.
Lynette:	Good afternoon. This is Lynette Peters calling. I'm trying to reach Mr. Donald Iverson who is scheduled to meet with Mr. Buracek at 4 p.m.
Buracek's secretary:	No, Mr. Iverson is not here.
Lynette:	Do you expect him?
Buracek's secretary:	You can call back.
Lynette:	I would like to leave a message…Hello?…Hello?

The phone hums, indicating that the connection has been broken.
Late afternoon in New Jersey, Donald calls Lynette.

Lynette:	I don't understand what happened this morning. I tried to leave a message for you at Mr. Buracek's office, but I was cut off.
Donald:	Oh, did his secretary hang up on you?
Lynette:	I think so. Why would she do that?

| Donald: | I forgot to warn you. Here in Russia they don't share our sense of telephone etiquette. They don't think to ask if you want to leave a message. Remember, under the Communist system there was very little business competition. People here haven't yet developed the habit of professional courtesy on the telephone. |

After the conversation with Donald, Lynette took out her personal international telephone notebook that she keeps at her desk. She made some notes concerning what to expect when making calls to Russia. Lynette understood that international communication requires knowledge in two major areas: 1) knowing the procedures for international calling and 2) understanding how to conduct intercultural communications.

Objectives

After completing this chapter, you should be able to:

- Locate information needed to place international telephone calls.
- Place international telephone calls using direct dialing or operator assistance.
- Identify translation services and devices.
- Calculate the time and date in foreign countries.
- Recognize the business factors and cultural characteristics that impact on intercultural communications.
- Understand the importance of overcoming language barriers and cultural differences in achieving successful intercultural communications.

International Calling Procedures

Thanks to technology, placing international calls to most places in the world is as easy as calling within the United States. There are more than 150 countries and locations outside the United States which can be dialed directly. For countries which cannot be reached through direct dialing, or when you have difficulty placing an overseas call, an operator will place the call for you.

LOCATING INFORMATION

The white pages telephone directory provided by your local telephone service carrier contains a listing of international country and city codes. Your long-distance telephone carrier may also be able to provide you with an international calling directory. Many desk calendars also include this kind of information. If you do not have access to a directory, you can dial 411 to get the information operator. The local information operator can also connect you to an international operator, if you do not have the telephone number of the company you are calling. Keep in mind that many local carriers charge for use of their information services.

You can save money for your company by looking up the information you need. If you need to locate the telephone number of an overseas company, you may be able to access it through a public library information service or a computerized on-line information service. Directories published by international trade associations and private firms also contain the names, addresses, and telephone numbers of companies and key personnel. **Trade associations** are organizations whose members are businesses and individuals within a particular industry, such as engineering, science, publishing, various kinds of manufacturing, and so on. You can contact the public library for a listing of organizations and directories in your field.

PLACING INTERNATIONAL CALLS

As mentioned previously, most international calls can be dialed direct. In some cases, you may need operator assistance. Before placing the call, make sure you have all the information you need so that you can conduct the business of your call as quickly as possible.

Direct Dial

For direct dialing, you need to dial 011 (the International Access Code), the country code, the city code, and the local number. For example, to place a direct-dial call to Rome, Italy:

011	39	6	_____
International Access Code	Country Code	City Code	Local Number

If you are calling collect or person-to-person, dial 01 instead of 011 for the International Access Code. When you have finished dialing, an operator will come on the line and ask what kind of assistance you need.

Operator-Assisted

If direct dialing is not available in the country you are calling or if you are experiencing difficulty dialing direct, an operator will place the call for you. For operator-assisted calls, dial 0 and tell the operator you wish to place an international call. You will be connected with an international operator. If you are experiencing difficulty, tell the operator the country and city code and the local number you are calling. If you are calling a country where direct dial is not available, give the name of the city and country and the local telephone number.

USING TRANSLATION SERVICES

If you place international calls regularly to the same companies, you will know whether or not the conversation can be conducted in English. If you are not sure whether or not English is spoken by the party you are calling, be prepared to handle the conversation in the language spoken in the country you are calling. If you do not speak the language yourself, you will need to arrange to have someone on the line who can translate for you. Telephone companies and telecommunications firms offer translation services for overseas calls. Most translation services employ interpreters who are familiar with terms used in business discussions. They can also identify what language is being spoken if you are not able to identify it or if you are not sure.

One example of a translation service is AT&T's Language Line. This service provides a toll-free number that allows callers to "conference in" an interpreter on any call by dialing an 800 number and requesting an interpreter. The request can be made prior to placing a call or after a conversation has been started, by using the telephone conference call feature. This is a 24-hour, seven-days-a-week service that provides interpreters in more than 140 languages.

Other telecommunications companies link callers who speak different languages with an interpreter through conference calling technology. You can check with your local or long-distance carrier to find out what options are available for translation services.

411

Wouldn't it be convenient to have a "talking translator" that fits into a briefcase or desk drawer to use whenever you need an interpreter? There is such a device that displays and translates a word or phrase into various languages, such as English, French, Spanish, Italian, and German. The user can key in a word, push the appropriate language key, and the computer translates the word through its speaker or earphone. A phrase button will activate a feature that scrolls through phrases that use a particular word. A device like the one shown in Figure 6-1 may have as many as 13,500 words and 60,000 phrases in its database. The device also pronounces the words in an authentic accent, so that you can use it to teach yourself to correctly speak the phrases you need.

Figure 6-1

The "talking translator" can be very helpful to businesspeople who have clients in many different countries.

CROSSING TIME ZONES

Being aware of differences in time is crucial to planning the right time to make international calls. Before you place an international call, be sure to check the time to make sure that it is during business hours in the country you are calling. For offices that are closed during the hours your office is open,

Figure 6-2

Consider each time zone when traveling around the world.

you might have to opt for communicating by air letter, overnight mail service, such as Federal Express, and fax. If telephone calls are absolutely necessary, you will need to arrange to make them outside of your normal office hours. For instance, if you are in California and need to speak with someone in London at 4 p.m. their time, you will need to call from your home or office at 6 a.m. your time.

If you make a lot of international calls, you will find it helpful to keep a notebook at your desk listing calling information such as telephone numbers, languages spoken, whether or not translation is needed, and any other notes that will assist you in making future calls. One item in this notebook should be a copy of a world time zone map. To use a world time zone map, subtract an hour for every time zone you cross going west and add one hour for every time zone you cross going east. For example, if you are calling from New York City at 9 a.m., it is 2 p.m. in London and 10 p.m. in Hong Kong.

You also need to be aware of the international dateline. The **international dateline** is an imaginary line along the 180th meridian, which is designated as the place where each calendar day begins. From the United States, countries east of the international dateline are a day ahead. For instance, when it is noon in New York, it is 2 a.m. the next day in Japan.

The following conversation illustrates how crossing time zones can affect international business communications. Howard Morrissey is arranging a business meeting in Okinawa for his boss, Ms. Jorgenson. He is speaking with Fumiko Yoshino, administrative assistant in the Japanese branch of his company.

Fumiko: You say that Ms. Jorgenson will be arriving tomorrow? What time tomorrow?

Howard: Her flight leaves Chicago at 7 a.m. on June 16. She lands in Japan at 9 a.m. on June 17.

Fumiko: No, she won't be here on the seventeenth, she'll be here on the eighteenth.

Howard: Oh, I guess so. Well, what time should she plan to arrive at your office tomorrow or the next day or whenever it is?

Fumiko: I will schedule her first appointment with the manufacturing group at 2 p.m. That will give Ms. Jorgenson some time to overcome her jet lag.

Howard: That's fine. Now, can you help me out? I'm confused about the time differences. Today is Monday, June 15, at 6 p.m. What's the date and time there? I want to make sure I get all the dates and times right on Ms. Jorgenson's itinerary.

1. Pretend that you are Fumiko and answer Howard's questions.

_____

2. Ms. Jorgenson wants to call home when she arrives in Japan. What time will it be in Chicago?

_____

_____

3. If Howard wants to contact Ms. Jorgenson at the Japanese firm just prior to her meeting, what time and date will he have to place his call from Chicago?

_____

_____

THE 24-HOUR CLOCK

The **24-hour clock** is sometimes referred to as military time in the United States because that is the setting in which it is most commonly used here. Outside of the United States, it is more commonly used to avoid confusion and reduce errors in identifying a.m. and p.m. The 24-hour clock shows the time with four digits, two for the hour and two for the minutes. The day begins at 0001 hours, which is one minute past midnight, and progresses through the day, ending at midnight, which is 2400 (stated as 24 hundred hours).

When you confront the need to use the 24-hour clock, just remember that morning hours are the same as on the 12-hour clock. For p.m. times, the simplest thing to do is to add 1200 to the hour. For example, 3 p.m. becomes 1500 hours. See Appendix C for a conversion chart and formula that you can tear out and keep for future use.

Intercultural Communications

Telecommunications technology has created the concept of the **global village,** in which we are all a part of one world community. Within this community, we are expected to be aware of and have respect for each other's cultural differences. In this sense, **culture** is used to mean the customary traits, attitudes, and behaviors of a group of people. Unless you are lucky enough to be a world traveler, you will need to make an effort to become familiar with the nuances involved in **intercultural communications,** which means communicating with people from other cultures outside of the United States. Even other English-speaking countries cannot be expected to have the same interpretation of our language, the same sense of humor, or the same everyday practices that we take for granted.

Areas of difference that affect international business the most are differences in business procedures, language barriers, and cultural characteristics.

INTERNATIONAL BUSINESS PROCEDURES

In most important ways, international businesses operate similarly to businesses in the United States. Some areas of difference you should be aware of are business hours, level of technological development, and business customs.

Business Hours

Hours of operation and days of the week that businesses are open vary around the world. For example, in Korea the workweek is Monday through Saturday and possibly Sunday. In some Middle Eastern countries, the workweek is Saturday through Wednesday, with Thursday and Friday off. Many countries close their offices in the middle of the day when the population takes its main meal and a midday rest. This is true, for example, in South America and Mexico, as well as Spain and Italy.

Technology

If you work in a high-tech office, don't assume that business associates around the world are operating in the same kind of environment. For instance, in many European countries telephone technology is not as advanced as in the United States. Many countries throughout the world do not have the sophisticated computer systems that we are starting to take for granted all over the United States. Be prepared to wait longer for information and don't expect everyone to be able to "look it up on the computer."

Business Customs

Here in the United States, we are known for our informality. This is true not only in how we casually address one another and exchange jokes, but also in how we approach doing business with our colleagues. We are prone to prioritize transactions and assign "understood" levels of importance to them. This mutual understanding allows us to handle many transactions by telephone with no written documentation. When communicating with international colleagues, you need to make sure you have the same understanding of what categories of business they expect to handle by telephone and what should be put in writing. You will probably find that more written correspondence is necessary with colleagues in other countries than is necessary for similar transactions in the United States.

Other areas where customs may differ include the amount of emphasis placed on the status of individuals within an organization and the importance of professional titles. The importance of using professional titles and the expression of a high degree of respect for those of higher status are customs of greater importance in many countries than they are in the United States. In the United States, it is quite common for employees of all ranks to be on a first-name basis with each other. Other countries, including European societies, tend to be more formal, addressing each other by title and last name. You are likely to encounter more formality between higher and lower status individuals and between members of the opposite sex.

The roles of women in business organizations vary also. In the United States, it is common to find women in high-ranking positions throughout the business world. In many regions of the world, such as the Middle East, Asia, and the Pacific Rim, women are not full participants in the business world or are only just beginning to move into high-level professional roles. When dealing with such cultures, it is important not to take offense overtly at what might be considered intolerable behavior by our standards. Most businesspeople around the world are becoming accustomed to finding women from the United States in responsible positions and know how to respond appropriately.

Figure 6-3

In the United States, women have a more prominent role in business than in many countries around the world.

ADJUSTING TO CULTURAL DIFFERENCES

When communicating interculturally, it is just as important to understand how you will be perceived as it is to be aware of your perceptions of others. Some cultural characteristics associated with people from the United States are that we are:

- Friendly and informal

- Impatient and time-conscious

- Insensitive to other cultures

- Direct in a polite way

- Individualistic

- Materialistic

As you broaden your awareness of the cultural characteristics of others, you will develop a sense of whether your cultural traits will be well-received or should be tempered to accommodate a different set of cultural norms. For example, in most other countries that U.S. companies do business with, including European countries and Japan, it is not the norm to use first names of persons whom you have just met. While directness in approaching business transactions is uncomfortable for the Japanese, it is the accepted style in Germany. Europeans are experienced in dealing with the directness of people from the United States, but over the telephone they prefer a brief period of social conversation preceding the business transaction. Developing the ability to pick up on these areas of subtle difference will make you more comfortable with intercultural communications.

Read the background information below. Then turn on your audiocassette player and listen to Audio Dialogue 6-1. Turn off the player when the end of the dialogue is announced. (Do not rewind the cassette.) Then answer the questions below.

Audio Dialogue 6-1

Background: Vernetta Davis has just been promoted to head of sales for the international marketing unit of Athletic Gear, Inc., a wholesale sales company. She is calling Saburo Fujiwara, the buyer at a Japanese department store, to renegotiate the terms of a contract. She has asked her assistant, Charles Franklin, to take part in the call so that he can read the contract changes to Mr. Fujiwara and make notes on the computer about any additional changes discussed in the conversation.

1. When Charles and Vernetta told Sam about their telephone conversation with Mr. Fujiwara, what do you think Sam told them about Japanese business culture in the following areas?

Audio Analysis 6-1

   a. Formality vs. informality when addressing colleagues:

   _____

   _____

b. Getting right down to business at the start of a conversation:

_____

_____

c. Being direct vs. being indirect:

_____

_____

d. The role of women in business:

_____

_____

e. The role of the individual vs. the group in making decisions:

_____

_____

_____

OVERCOMING LANGUAGE BARRIERS

There are 3,000 different languages spoken throughout the world. English speakers are lucky in that English is the international business language. When talking with non-native English speakers, you need to be aware that their sense of humor and understanding of slang is likely to be different from yours. Until you get to know someone, it is best to avoid trying to make jokes over the telephone.

When you are speaking with a non-native English speaker, remember that English is a second language for that person. Don't expect everyone who speaks English to be completely fluent in the language. Avoid judging a lack of fluency as an indication of a lack of intelligence. Generally, you will use the same techniques discussed in Chapter 3 to enhance your communications skills. To assist with understanding, keep the following in mind:

- Use simple words and short, clear phrases and sentences.

- Enunciate clearly and pace your speech so that it can be easily understood. Do not speak so slowly that you insult the other person's intelligence.

- Avoid slang words, business jargon, and colloquial expressions altogether, rather than risk being misunderstood.

Most people from other countries are appreciative if you try to use a few words to communicate with them in their language, even though the rest of the conversation will be conducted in English. Learning to greet your international business colleagues in their native language can help establish a good working relationship. It is easy to learn simple phrases in other languages or keep a list in your notebook. Don't hesitate to ask for assistance in pronunciation.

Some basic words and phrases are translated in the table below:

	Japanese	**Spanish**	**French**	**German**
Good morning	Ohayo gozaimasu	Buenos dias	Bon jour	Guten morgen
Good evening or Good night	Konban wa	Buenas noches	Bon soir	Guten nacht
How are you?	Ogenki desuka?	Como esta usted?	Comment allez-vous?	Wie geht es ihnen?
Thank you	Arigato	Gracias	Merci	Danke
Good bye	Sayonara	Adios	Au revoir	Auf wiedersehen

LEARNING ABOUT OTHER CULTURES

If you are interested in pursuing a career in international business or working with a multinational company, you will need to acquire as much knowledge as possible about the international community. One thing that offends people in international communications is ignorance of basic facts about their country. Knowing the geographic location, climate, and most commonly spoken languages of a country are the basics that you need in order to function in an international business setting. When you converse with people in other countries, it is important to know something about their political situation, their holidays, and any important cultural factors, such as religion, that affect their everyday lives. One of the easiest and least expensive ways to learn about other countries is by reading magazine and newspaper articles. Keeping up with international news by reading a weekly news magazine, watching international news programs and specials, or reading the international news in the daily newspaper will help you stay informed. Travel books and the travel sections of major newspapers like the Sunday edition of the *New York Times* are also good sources of information.

Many books have been written on the subject of international business and intercultural communications. Educational institutions and business training programs also offer opportunities for short and long courses on international business. There are also consulting groups and professionals who offer workshops and seminars for those who want to learn more about intercultural communications.

No matter what your level of knowledge is, the best way to deal with intercultural communications is to be open and accepting of other cultures. Depending on your level of prior exposure to a particular country or region, you will bring a certain level of discomfort to your initial contacts. For example, you may be happy to find that a contact speaks English, but at the same time be embarrassed that you cannot communicate in the other person's language. As long as you are open and accepting of other cultures and have a willingness to learn, you will become more and more confident as your experience grows through participation in the global village.

Chapter Summary

■ International calls can be placed through direct dial or through operator assistance. Numbers for international country and city codes can be found in your local telephone directory. Other sources are international calling directories, desk references, and the information operator.

■ You can arrange to have a translator on the line during international calls. Telephone companies and telecommunications firms offer translation services.

■ Crossing time zones when making international calls requires careful planning. Calls must be made during the appropriate business hours in the country being contacted.

■ The international dateline is the designated place where each calendar day begins. Countries east of the international dateline are a day ahead of countries west of the dateline.

■ When conducting international communications, it is important to be aware of cultural differences that have an impact on business procedures, language usage, and attitudes and behaviors of people with whom you interact.

■ Language barriers can occur with non-native English speakers if you use slang, jargon, or colloquial expressions which they may not understand.

■ Even if your international colleagues speak English, it is a good idea to learn a few words in their language and acquire some knowledge about things of interest in their country.

Key Terms

culture

direct dial

global village

intercultural communications

international dateline

operator-assisted calls

trade association

24-hour clock

Chapter Review

Write your answers to the questions that follow and be prepared to discuss them in class.

1. **What sources can you use to locate information needed to place international telephone calls? Why is it best to look up information rather than use directory assistance or the operator?**

    _____

    _____

    _____

2. **Some common business customs in U.S. companies are listed below. Consult some sources of information, such as books, articles, or persons who are involved in international business. Research three countries that interest you and find out whether their customs are the same or different.**

    a. **Work hours are 9 a.m. to 5 p.m.**

    b. **Workers are allowed to take one 15-minute break in the morning and one in the afternoon.**

    c. **Workers have an hour off for lunch.**

    d. **Hourly employees are paid for overtime.**

    e. **Offices provide employee services such as a cafeteria, lounges, a medical office, and a gym.**

    f. **Offices have designated smoking areas, or no smoking is allowed on the premises.**

3. **Assume that you have a job that requires you to call branch offices located in various parts of the world. You want to set up a schedule for making three of the calls on Friday morning and three on Friday afternoon. All of your branch offices are open from 9 a.m. to 5 p.m. local time, Monday through Friday. Based on the time zone where you live, write down the best time for you to schedule calls to the countries listed and what time you should tell the person you are calling to be available.**

    Germany _____

    Australia _____

Brazil _____

Japan _____

Ghana _____

The Phillipines _____

4. **Sports is an international pastime that people from all countries can relate to. If you wanted to chat with international business colleagues about sports, what sports would people from the following countries be interested in? If you don't know, do some research or ask someone who is familiar with these places:**

Canada _____

Switzerland _____

Venezuela _____

Spain _____

France _____

5. **Page 99 lists some cultural traits that are associated with people from the United States. For each trait listed below, list some behaviors of yourself or others you know that contribute to this image of Americans.**

Friendly and informal:

_____

_____

Impatient and time-conscious:

_____

_____

Insensitive to other cultures:

_____

_____

Direct in a polite way:

_____

_____

Individualistic:

_____

_____

Materialistic:

_____

_____

Audio Dialogue 6-2

Read the background information below. Then turn on your audiocassette player and listen to Audio Dialogue 6-2. Turn off the player when the end of the dialogue is announced. (Do not rewind the cassette.) Then answer the questions below.

Background: Alexander Bennington is planning to attend a convention of the International Society of Information Managers. The members of this organization work in the computer field, helping companies convert their paper records to electronic storage systems. The convention is being held in Sydney, Australia, from February 9-12. Alexander is speaking to Jennifer Woods, the convention coordinator, to finalize his reservations for the conference.

Audio Analysis 6-2

1. It takes 26 hours to fly from the East Coast of the United States to Australia. Suggest a convenient time and date for Alexander to leave in order to arrive in time to rest in the afternoon before attending the reception at 6 p.m. on February 8.

_____

_____

2. What is some basic information that Alexander could have found out about Australia that would have helped to avoid problems when planning his trip and packing?

_____

_____

_____

3. Did Alexander cause miscommunication to occur because of inattention to his use of language? If so, site the words or phrases that created a problem.

_____

_____

_____

4. From Jennifer's conversation about the reception, what conclusions might Alexander draw about the Australians' and Spaniards' viewpoints on punctuality?

_____

_____

_____

TELEMARKETING

Chapter

7

On the Job: Using Telephone Skills to Sell

Lenora Williams is excited that she was called for a second job interview with Worldclass Software, a mail-order software company. She hopes to be hired for a position as a customer service helpline operator. She feels that this is the perfect opportunity to build on the skills she developed as a customer service representative at a large computer store.

The human resources director, Herb Caldwell, greets her and shows her into his office. "Hello, Lenora. It's nice to see you again."

"Thank you," Lenora replies. "I'm eager to hear about my test results and how I did on the interview."

"You did very well on both. We're also impressed with your references and your demonstrated skill in working with customers. In fact, Lenora, if you're interested, we'd like to consider you for a different position with Worldclass Software. We're expanding our telemarketing sales operation, and, we'd like you to consider joining our training program to become a telemarketing representative."

"Well, I know I'm qualified to work the helpline. I'm used to dealing with customers' questions and problems. But what would I do as a telemarketing representative?"

"As a telemarketing representative, you will be the one to initiate contact with the customer to generate sales, as opposed to working with customers who contact you after making a purchase. Our expanded operation will be used to reach current customers to try to get them to buy new products. We're planning to concentrate at first on the small business and consumer markets. We've been using our information system to compile profiles of our customers. You would use this information to target specific customers for new products based on their previous buying patterns and the type of work they do."

"So in addition to learning product information, I would also learn to use a computerized customer information system. What about the selling part?"

"You would attend a five-day in-house training program that covers all aspects of telemarketing sales. We will then assign an experienced sales representative to work with you your first two weeks. For the following two weeks, a supervisor will be on the line to help you handle calls. If you're interested in exploring this further, I can make an appointment for you to meet with the head of the telemarketing department later this week."

"Yes, I am interested. I feel I would need to learn more about what telemarketing is and what would be expected of me."

"Good. Then we'll set up the appointment and go from there."

Lenora has been offered an opportunity to use her past work experience in a growing field that offers many career opportunities. Businesses and other types of organizations are expanding their use of telemarketing for sales, customer service, market research, and other functions that can be handled in a time- and cost-effective way by using telecommunications technology.

Objectives

After completing this chapter, you should be able to:

- Explain the key aspects of telemarketing sales and how they are used in the selling process.

- Identify key steps in the selling process and explain the purpose of each step.

- Evaluate a sales call and make recommendations for improvement.

- Recognize different types of telephone market research and explain the processes they employ.

- Explain how telemarketing is used in the field of fund-raising and demonstrate successful techniques.

- Identify job opportunities in the field of telemarketing.

- Understand the importance of ethics and professionalism in the telemarketing field and gain an awareness of the industry standards.

■ The Telemarketing Concept

Almost everyone has experienced telemarketing from the receiving end. Out of the blue, someone calls and asks you to make a purchase, contribute to a cause, or renew a subscription. **Telemarketing** is the use of telecommunications and information systems to sell products and services and maintain or establish contact with present and potential customers. It is also a method of conducting market research and fund-raising.

Figure 7-1

Large companies use telemarketing to sell products and to maintain customer contact.

Courtesy of Lillian Vernon

TYPES OF TELEMARKETING

When a telemarketer initiates a call to a customer, this is called **proactive telemarketing.** Companies of all sizes use this technique to follow up with current customers and reach potential new customers.

Sometimes proactive telemarketing is used in conjunction with **personal selling,** which is a face-to-face sales encounter. The telephone call may follow a personal visit by a sales representative. Other companies find it effective to use telemarketing exclusively to sell their products and services or to combine telemarketing with direct mail. **Direct mail** may be a printed brochure, letter, catalog, postcard, or product sample sent to prospective customers. The mailing is followed up with a call. Another technique is to use telemarketing to identify interested customers and then follow up with direct mail information.

Companies also take advantage of telemarketing to get reactions to new products, to push products that are not cost-effective for personal selling, and to reach customers in regions that are beyond the scope of their personal selling sales force.

With the explosion of 800 and 900 numbers, television home shopping services, catalog shopping, and computerized shopping services, more and more customers are initiating the use of telemarketing services. It is estimated that the Home Shopping Network receives up to 100,000 calls per day. When the customer initiates the call, the service is called **reactive telemarketing.** Some

companies have representatives available to take customers' calls 24 hours a day. The advantage of reactive telemarketing is that when the customer initiates the contact, the representative does not have to meet with any immediate resistance. However, the customer has certain expectations that must be met in order for resistance not to set in. When customers reach an automated attendant, they expect quick, logical instructions. Customers also want contact with representatives who are able to answer questions about products, delivery schedules, prices, and follow-up in case of problems with the order.

Information systems are a major part of the telemarketing function. The ability of telemarketers to instantly access a database of customer information while interacting with customers on the phone enables companies to better serve customers. Companies compile data and create **customer profiles**, a set of characteristics common to specified groupings such as age, income, and educational background. Customer profiles are used for **market segmentation**, a categorizing of markets used to target those customers that are most likely to respond positively to a particular kind of call.

TELEMARKETING SKILLS

All the telephone skills discussed in earlier chapters will be applied to telemarketing work. The communications skills that companies consider most important in the telemarketing function are:

- A clear, pleasantly modulated voice

- The ability to be persistent, but not insistent, in persuading the customer

- The ability to accept rejection and remain motivated

- The ability to project an enthusiastic, friendly telephone personality and to sound sincere

- The ability to adapt to different types of customers and handle new situations

- The ability to organize and present information and respond to questions

Most companies give telemarketing employees extensive training. Training programs usually include an orientation to the company's business functions, specific product knowledge, sales techniques, and practice in handling different kinds of customers and situations. Other areas of training may include organizational and time-management skills.

USES OF TELEMARKETING

Telemarketing is used most frequently for direct sales. Other important uses include market research and fund-raising.

Sales. Selling, taking orders, upgrading orders; generating, screening, and qualifying leads.

Market Research. Conducting **market surveys** by questioning a large cross section of people, and gathering information by interviewing customers and potential customers.

Fund-Raising. Soliciting contributions for charities and other types of non-profit organizations.

These three functions are covered in this chapter. Customer service is also a key telemarketing function. Because of its importance, this subject is covered separately in Chapter 8.

◼ Telemarketing Sales

Thousands of books have been written on the art and skill of selling. It is a complex process that requires training, skill, and persistence. Even experienced salespersons need some customer orientation and product knowledge when going into a new situation. Most companies require formal training before a telemarketer gets on the phone and tries to sell. In the course of training, employees practice their speaking skills, their ability to explain the product or service, and their ability to answer questions.

KEY ASPECTS OF SELLING

Some key aspects of the selling process that are emphasized in training programs are: explaining customer benefits, overcoming objections, closing the sale, and handling rejection.

Explaining Benefits
Telemarketers are trained to present a clear explanation of the benefits of the product or service they are selling. **Benefits** are the advantages to the customer if the purchase is made, such as "Taking advantage of our offer will cost you $50 less than if you purchased the item in a department store." In addition to price, benefits are often explained in terms of comparison to competing products,

appeals to the customers' emotions, or appeals to the customers' desire to have the "newest," the "most up-to-date," or the "most popular" product.

Overcoming Objections

Objections are the customers' stated reasons for saying no. When a company has a great deal of experience in selling a product, objections can be anticipated. Telemarketers can be trained to give specific responses that have been used with other customers to overcome the objection. With new products, telemarketers make notes of objections and develop a set of responses over time.

Closing the Sale

The sale **closing** takes place when the telemarketer asks directly for the sale. This step should not come too early or too late in the process. Training programs teach telemarketers to pick up on cues that indicate when the customer is ready to make the commitment. A cue might be a change in the level of the objection from a major issue to a minor issue or questions about price before the telemarketer has reached that point in the presentation.

Handling Rejection

Another key aspect of sales is dealing with rejection. This is something that proactive salespersons confront on a regular basis. Learning to take rejection in stride is a key to successful selling. The beginning salesperson has to continually assess his or her technique after each rejection. It is also important to examine the customers' stated reasons for saying no. For instance, often people are reluctant to admit that price is an issue and will set up other barriers instead. With experience, salespersons learn to probe beyond stated objections so that they are not left wondering why they lost a sale. In most telemarketing operations, supervisors monitor calls and offer coaching to correct problems in presentation techniques.

THE SEVEN-STEP SELLING PROCESS

In their book, *Successful Telemarketing,* Bob Stone and John Wyman outline a selling process that has been used successfully by AT&T Communications. This process emphasizes another key aspect of selling, sometimes called **preselling,** which involves identifying the customer's need through the use of questioning techniques. This element is particularly applicable to situations where products have not been targeted to specific customers through techniques such as customer profiling.

The Seven-Step Selling Process [1]

1. Precall Planning
   a. Review customer information
   b. Plan objective of the call
   c. Psych yourself—get mentally ready for the call!

2. Approach/Positioning
   a. Identify who you are and whom you represent

[1] Bob Stone and John Wyman, *Successful Telemarketing: Opportunities and Techniques for Increasing Sales and Profits* (Lincolnwood, Illinois: NTC Business Books, 1992). Adapted with permission.

    b. Explain the purpose of the call

    c. Get through the receptionist/screener

    d. Get the decision-maker

    e. Make an interest-creating statement

    f. Build rapport

3. Data Gathering

    a. Gain a general understanding of the customer's business

    b. Use questioning techniques

    c. Move from general to specific questions

    d. Identify a customer business need

4. Solution Generation

    a. Tailor the solution to a specific customer need

    b. Ask in-depth questions to test the feasibility of the solution

    c. Gather data for cost/benefit analysis

    d. Prepare the customer for the recommendation

5. Solution Presentation

    a. Get the customer's agreement to the area of need

    b. Present recommendation in a clear and concise manner

    c. Explain benefits

6. Close

    a. Know when to close

    b. Understand buying signals

    c. Overcome objections

    d. Use close techniques

7. Wrap-Up

    a. Discuss implementation issues

    b. Thank the customer for the business

    c. Confirm the customer's commitment

    d. Leave name and number

    e. Position for the next call

Following is an example of how a telemarketer for L.L.M. Pharmaceuticals, a wholesaler of veterinary drugs, used the seven-step technique:

1. Precall planning. The telemarketer reviews the account file of the Whiteside Veterinary Clinic. He notes that Dr. Sargent ordered her usual order of drug supplies last month, but that she hasn't tried a new drug that L.L.M. Pharmaceuticals has recently introduced via direct mail.

    The telemarketer reviews his introduction briefly, takes a deep breath, and says, "Smile!"

2. Approach/positioning. "Hello. This is Mark Wiley with L.L.M. Pharmaceuticals. Dr. Sargent is usually available about this time. May I speak with her?"

    "Good morning, Dr. Sargent. This is Mark Wiley with L.L.M. How have things been going at your clinic since I last talked to you? (Pause) I'm certainly glad to hear that! Dr. Sargent, as a buyer of many of our quality products, I knew you'd be interested in hearing about one of our innovative new drugs. If you have a minute, I'd like to ask you a couple of questions. . . ."

3. **Data gathering.** "Doctor, your practice pretty much covers a suburban area, doesn't it?"

   "Right now when a dog is suffering from hookworm, what drug are you prescribing?"

4. **Solution generation.** "Many vets also used to prescribe that particular drug. Have you had many dogs suffering from various side effects from that drug?"

   "Would you be interested in prescribing a new drug that has few, if any, side effects?"

5. **Solution presentation.** "L.L.M. has introduced Formula XYZ that not only has fewer side effects, but extensive laboratory tests have shown that the medicine takes effect 24 hours more quickly than similar drugs."

6. **Close.** "I'm sure that your customers would appreciate faster relief for their pets. Can I add a case of Formula XYZ to your regular order?"

7. **Wrap-up.** "I'm sure that you will be pleased with the results, Dr. Sargent. We've gotten excellent comments back from many vets around the country. I'll get that shipment to you by early next week. Thank you for your business. I'll be calling you again the first of next month. Have a good day!"[2]

1. What major objection did Mark anticipate from the customer and overcome in his presentation?

   _____

   _____

2. What product benefits did Mark present to the customer?

   _____

   _____

   _____

3. How did Mark directly ask for the sale?

   _____

   _____

   _____

Audio Dialogue 7-1

Read the background information below. Then turn on your audiocassette player and listen to Audio Dialogue 7-1. Turn off the player when the end of the dialogue is announced. (Do not rewind the cassette.) Then answer the questions on the following page.

Background: Lenora Williams was hired by Worldclass Software and has entered the training program to become a telemarketing sales representative. She has completed the classroom training and is now in the on-the-job training phase of the program. This morning she is calling customers who have already

[2]Ibid. Used with permission.

purchased Financial Wiz, a computerized record-keeping program. She is now trying to sell them a new program, called Tax Accountant, that will organize and prepare records for income tax preparation. Lenora's supervisor, Alex Kramer, is listening in on the call and will discuss his evaluation with Lenora.

Below is the evaluation form that Alex Kramer used as he listened to Lenora's sales call. Pretend that you are Alex and complete the evaluation checklist. Use the seven-step selling process as a guideline. Discuss your evaluation with members of the class.

Audio Analysis 7-1

EVALUATION CHECKLIST

1. Approach/Positioning
   ____ Identified herself
   ____ Explained the purpose of the call
   ____ Got the decision-maker
   ____ Created interest and built rapport
   Rating: Good ____Fair ____Needs Improvement ____

2. Data Gathering
   ____ Used questioning techniques to gain understanding of customer's business
   ____ Moved from general to specific questions
   ____ Identified customer's need
   Rating: Good ____Fair ____Needs Improvement ____

3. Solution Generation
   ____ Tailored solution to customer's need
   ____ Asked questions to test feasibility of the solution
   ____ Gathered cost/benefit data
   ____ Prepared customer for the recommendation
   Rating: Good ____Fair ____Needs Improvement ____

4. Solution Presentation
   ____ Got customer's agreement to area of need
   ____ Presented recommendation
   ____ Explained benefits
   Rating: Good ____Fair ____Needs Improvement ____

5. Close
   ____ Knew when to close
   ____ Understood buying signals
   ____ Overcame objections
   Rating: Good ____Fair ____Needs Improvement ____

6. Wrap-Up
   ____ Discussed implementation (follow-up) issues
   ____ Thanked customer for the business
   ____ Confirmed the customer's commitment
   ____ Left name and number
   ____ Positioned for the next call
   Rating: Good ____Fair ____Needs Improvement ____

Market Research

Telemarketing is used to gather information that companies need to market their products and services in the most effective way. In its simplest form, **market research** is just a matter of asking questions in an efficient and polite manner at the end of a sales call. This is called **point-of-sale market research.** For more formal research, a telephone survey is used. A **telephone survey** is a prepared set of questions used to conduct an interview. Formal surveys are not normally a part of a sales call.

POINT-OF-SALE MARKET RESEARCH

An ideal time to gather information is right after completing a sale to a customer. A customer who has just called to hire a cleaning service may be asked, "How did you find out about our service?" This helps the company find out whether their space ads in local newspapers, flyers sent through the mail, or word of mouth from satisfied customers is the most effective way to attract new business. A telemarketer of a product that frequently runs out of inventory may ask customers who order in bulk, "Approximately how many boxes of computer paper does your office use per month?"

The point-of-sale technique can also be used to generate leads. The telemarketer may ask, "Do you have any friends who might be interested in receiving information about our products?" It can also be used to identify customer needs or problems. For example, a customer who has placed a smaller than usual order to a wholesaler might be asked if the customer is having trouble moving the product and if so, why. If there is less demand for the product, the telemarketer might suggest a small order of a different product for a trial run.

It is important that the telemarketer plan what information-gathering questions are going to be asked and refrain from engaging in a lengthy discussion.

Figure 7-3

Telemarketers need an organized set of questions that can be answered by checking off items on a questionnaire.

Customers will not mind being kept on the telephone for a short period of time to offer helpful information. However, a lengthy discussion would be an imposition on the customer which may lead to negative feelings at the end of the call.

For some telemarketers, information gathering is an assigned part of the job. In other cases, it is something that the telemarketer does on his or her own initiative. Whether or not information gathering is an assigned task, it is a good idea to keep a written record of the customers' responses. A specific documentation of how many calls were made, how many customers were questioned, and the specific responses is much more useful to the sales representative and to the company than a general conclusion such as, "Most of my customers are not interested in that product any more."

TELEPHONE SURVEYS

Formal market research is the most effective tool in a company's ongoing efforts to live up to the business principle of "know your customer." This type of call takes time and, therefore, it is made strictly for that purpose. Customers who have time are usually pleased to participate in such surveys because they welcome the opportunity to state their feelings and opinions. Some of the uses of telephone survey information are to:

- Improve products or services

- Get ideas for developing new products or services

- Get reactions to newly released products

- Develop better telephone dialogues for future sales calls

- Improve company procedures for processing orders or delivering goods and services

A telephone survey begins with the development of a questionnaire. The questions should be kept to a minimum and should be clearly focused on the objective of the survey. While the survey will have several questions, it's overall purpose should be to answer only one question, such as "What is the profile of a typical customer?" or "Given our typical customer, will we get a greater response to an ad campaign placed on television, radio, or in a weekly news magazine?"

In order to conduct the survey efficiently and not waste either the telemarketer's or the customers' time, the survey questions should be in multiple-choice or short-answer format. Open-ended questions are difficult to answer and do not provide quantitative data that can be easily analyzed. Depending on how complex the issue, telephone surveys are sometimes followed up by in-depth interviews of participants.

Following is a sample telephone survey questionnaire.

Objective: Will Channel 57 Viewers Who Watch in Prime Time Use a Home Shopping Service?

Hello, this is _____, calling from WTUV, channel 57 on your cable TV service. We are planning to provide cable TV viewers with a new shopping service. Do you have a few minutes to answer some questions that will help us determine whether our customers would use this service?

1. First, do you watch channel 57 between the hours of 6 p.m. and 10 p.m.?
   _____ Yes (go to question 2)
   _____ No (go to question 3)

2. How often do you watch programming on channel 57?
   _____ More than five days a week
   _____ Two or three days a week
   _____ Less than one day a week

3. Would you be inclined to watch channel 57 between the hours of 6 p.m. and 10 p.m. if it offered a home shopping service during commercial breaks?
   _____ Yes
   _____ No

4. Are you presently taking advantage of any of the home shopping services available on cable TV?
   _____ Yes
   _____ No (THANK CALLER AND END)

5. Would you describe your purchases as
   _____ Frequent (several times per month)
   _____ Fairly frequent (more than once per month)
   _____ Infrequent (less than once per month)

6. Which of the following amounts do you spend on an average purchase of home shopping merchandise?
   _____ $50 or less
   _____ Between $50 and $100
   _____ Between $100 and $500

7. What are three items that you have purchased from a home shopping service in the past year?
   1. _____
   2. _____
   3. _____

8. How would you describe your feelings about your purchases?
   _____ Satisfied
   _____ Fairly satisfied
   _____ Dissatisfied
   If dissatisfied: Did you return any of the items?
   _____ Yes
   _____ No

THANK YOU FOR YOUR HELP. MAY WE CONTACT YOU AGAIN FOR A FOLLOW-UP INTER-VIEW?

_____ Yes

_____ No

INTERVIEWER _____

DATE _____

TIME _____

Some things to remember when developing a telephone survey:

- Questions should be focused only on issues that relate to the overall objective.

- Questions and answer choices should be short and stated in clear language. Avoid use of company or industry jargon that may confuse the customer.

- Questions should be worded objectively; that is, they should not lead off with preconceived conclusions or loaded words that influence the customer's response.

- Answer choices should be limited and offer realistic responses. Respondents should be allowed to supply their own answers where appropriate.

Some things to keep in mind when conducting a telephone survey:

- Do not mislead people as to the length of time it will take.

- Do not waste time with people who want to chat; comment politely on side remarks and then firmly move on to the next question.

- Be familiar with the questionnaire so that you can move quickly from marking an answer to stating the next question.

- Never tell a customer that you are calling to conduct market research and then end the conversation with trying to make a sale.

411

ProPhone™, The National Telephone Directory on CD-ROM™, is a nationwide telephone directory. By keying in a name, street address, ZIP code, or area code, the user can get listings from telephone directories across the nation. Listings can also be accessed by type of business. For instance, a user could call up names of all the caterers within a particular area code or ZIP code. Some things the user can do with ProPhone include:

- Browse through 77 million records from 10,000 phone books.

- View all listings for any type of business nationwide, statewide, or locally.

- Identify the size of a market and create lists of prospects.

- Create mailing labels from the data.

Fund-Raising

Each year thousands of private organizations solicit funds for charities, the arts, disaster relief, community and educational programs, and many other causes. It is estimated that charitable organizations collect billions of dollars annually. Organizations that use telemarketing to solicit funds are finding that telephone campaigns raise larger amounts of money than direct-mail campaigns. Telemarketing is particularly effective when targeted to a specifically defined group, such as people who have made previous contributions or given to similar causes.

FUND-RAISING TECHNIQUES

Some basic techniques of fund-raising that produce successful results include:

- Identify a target group which has made contributions to your cause or similar causes in the past. Since nonprofit organizations are tax-exempt, their donors' names must be made public.

- Be as specific as possible about the project and how the funds will be used.

- Be prepared to confirm the legitimacy of the organization to the donor.

- Suggest specific contribution amounts to new contributors.

- Mention the past amount given by prior contributors and request a specific increase over the last contribution.

THE FUND-RAISING PROCESS

Some of the steps telemarketers employ in the fund-raising process include the following:

Identify the organization. For new contributors, ask if the respondent is familiar with the organization and its cause. If the answer is "No," the telemarketer then reads a brief written description. If the answer is "Yes," the telemarketer responds by saying something like, "Then you are probably aware that…"

and then reads the prepared description to ensure that the respondent really does understand the nature of the organization. Here is an example of a description: "The Young People's Foundation for the Homeless has been in existence for the past two years. We are a nonprofit organization that supplies meals to homeless people on Saturdays and Sundays. Local public schools donate their premises, and students volunteer to serve the meals. Each week we provide meals to several hundred needy people all over the city."

Identify the purpose of the call. "In order to keep the program going, we rely on private donations from people in the community. Your contribution would be used to purchase food, supplies, and provide transportation for people who need help in getting to the program sites."

Make a direct request. "Would you be willing to make a contribution of $25, $35, or $50 today?"

Alter the request if necessary. "Even $5 or $10 would make a difference in the number of people who could be helped by our program. Can you make a $5 or $10 contribution today?"

Sign-off to a positive response. "Thank you very much for your time and for your donation. We will send a follow-up card in the mail for you to return with your donation. Could I please have your address?"

Sign-off to a negative response. "Thank you anyway for your time. Perhaps you will be able to help at us at a later date. Good-bye."

 # The Telemarketing Field

In many businesses, the telemarketing function is an integral part of the overall sales and marketing functions. The telemarketer's job may center on following up on leads generated by field sales representatives, advertisements, and promotional campaigns. In some companies, generating sales through telemarketing is a major operation carried out by a large in-house staff. Telephone service organizations, catalog sales companies, and fund-raising organizations are good examples of this type of operation.

With the increased recognition of the benefits of telemarketing, organizations that provide this service to other companies are on the increase. These organizations are called **telemarketing service bureaus** or **telemarketing agencies.** Some of these organizations simply handle telephone inquiries and orders (reactive telemarketing). Others develop and maintain complete telemarketing programs on a fee-paid service basis. Some telemarketing service organizations are highly sophisticated. They offer special expertise in maintaining extensive customer information through the use of automation. They can advise a company on how to use a telemarketing program to increase sales, as well as how to design and operate the program.

The field of telemarketing is recognized as requiring a high degree of ethics and professionalism. When customers are turned off by telemarketing calls from one company, they may become generally unreceptive to telephone solicitation. Many companies follow the guidelines for telephone marketing practice established by the Direct Marketing Association, Inc., a professional trade organization that monitors standards in the field of marketing.

Guidelines for Marketing by Telephone[3]

PROMPT DISCLOSURE/IDENTITY OF SELLER

Article 1

When speaking with a customer, telephone marketers should promptly disclose the name of the sponsor, the name of the individual caller, and the primary purposes of the contact.

All documents relating to a telephone marketing offer and shipment should sufficiently identify the full name and street address of the seller so that the customer may contact the seller by mail or by telephone.

HONESTY

Article 2

All offers should be clear, honest, and complete so that the customer will know the exact nature of what is being offered and the commitment involved in the placing of an order. Before making an offer, telephone marketers should be prepared to substantiate any claims or offers made. Advertisements or specific claims which are untrue, misleading, deceptive, fraudulent, or unjustly disparaging of competitors should not be used.

No one should make offers or solicitations in the guise of research or a survey when the real intent is to sell products or services or to raise funds.

TERMS OF THE OFFER

Article 3

Prior to commitments by customers, telephone marketers should disclose the cost of the merchandise or service and all terms and conditions, including payment plans, refund policies, and the amount or existence of any extra charges such as shipping and handling and insurance.

REASONABLE HOURS

Article 4

Telephone marketers should avoid making contacts during hours which are unreasonable to the recipients of the calls.

USE OF AUTOMATIC EQUIPMENT

Article 5

When using automatic dialing equipment, telephone marketers should only use equipment which allows the telephone immediately to release the line when the called party disconnects.

ARMPS (Automatic Recorded Message Players) and prerecorded messages should be used only in accordance with tariffs, state and local laws, and these Guidelines. When a telephone marketer places a call to a customer for solicitation purposes, and desires to deliver a recorded message, permission should be

[3]Direct Marketing Association, Inc., Guidelines for Marketing by Telephone. (Washington, D.C. 1993)

obtained from the customer by a live "operator" before the recorded message is delivered.

TAPING OF CONVERSATIONS
Article 6
Taping of telephone conversations made for telephone marketing purposes should not be conducted without legal notice to or consent of all parties or the use of a beeping device.

NAME REMOVAL
Article 7
Telephone marketers should remove the name of any individual from their telephone lists when requested directly to do so by the customer, by use of the DMA Telephone Preference Service name-removal list and, when applicable, the DMA Mail Preference Service name-removal list.

MINORS
Article 8
Because minors are generally less experienced in their rights as consumers, telephone marketers should be especially sensitive to the obligations and responsibilities involved when dealing with them. Offers suitable only for adults should not be made to children.

MONITORING
Article 9
Monitoring of telephone marketing and customer relations conversations should be conducted only after employees have been informed of the practice.

PROMPT DELIVERY
Article 10
Telephone marketers should abide by the FTC's Mail Order Merchandise (Thirty-Day) Rule when shipping prepaid merchandise. As a normal business procedure, telephone marketers are urged to ship all orders as soon as practical.

COOLING-OFF PERIOD
Article 11
Telephone marketers should honor cancellation requests that originate within three days of sales agreements.

RESTRICTED CONTACTS
Article 12
Telephone marketers should remove the name of any customer from their telephone lists when requested by the individual. Marketers should use the DMA Telephone Preference Service name-removal list and, when applicable, the DMA Mail Preference Service name-removal list. Names found on such suppression lists should not be rented, sold, or exchanged except for suppression purposes.

A telephone marketer should not knowingly call anyone who has an unlisted or unpublished telephone number except in instances when the number was provided by the customer to that marketer.

Random dialing techniques, whether manual or automated, in which identification of those parties called is left to chance, should not be used in sales and marketing solicitations.

Sequential dialing techniques, whether a manual or automated process, in which selection of those parties to be called is based on the location of their telephone numbers in a sequence of telephone numbers, should not be used.

TRANSFER OF DATA
Article 13
Telephone marketers who receive or collect customer data as a result of a telephone marketing contact, and who intend to rent, sell, or exchange those data for direct marketing purposes, should inform the customer. Customer requests regarding restrictions on the collection, rental, sale, or exchange of data relating to them should be honored.

Names on the DMA Telephone Preference Service name-removal list should not be transferred except for suppression purposes.

LAWS, CODES, AND REGULATIONS
Article 14
Telephone marketers should operate in accordance with the laws and regulations of the United States Postal Service, the Federal Communications Commission, the Federal Trade Commission, the Federal Reserve Board, and other applicable federal, state, and local laws governing advertising, marketing practices, and the transaction of business by mail, telephone, and the print and broadcast media.

Chapter Summary

- Telemarketing is the use of telecommunications and information systems to sell products and services and maintain or establish contact with present and potential customers.

- Proactive telemarketing occurs when a company initiates a call to a customer. When the customer initiates the call in response to an ad or a catalog, for instance, this is known as reactive telemarketing.

- Telemarketing companies use customer profiles and market segmentation to target their marketing efforts.

- Important skills for telemarketers are selling, persistence, resilience, enthusiasm, adaptability, and organization.

- Key aspects of the selling process that most telemarketers cover in training programs are explaining benefits, overcoming objections, closing the sale, and handling rejection.

- The elements of the seven-step selling process are precall planning, approach/positioning, data gathering, solution generation, solution presentation, close, and wrap-up.

- Point-of-sale market research takes place when customers are asked to answer a few brief questions and is often conducted at the end of a sales call.

- Telemarketers conduct telephone surveys separately from sales calls. The telemarketer usually has a written questionnaire to use as a guide during the survey.

- Telemarketing is often used by nonprofit groups for fund-raising. Some effective fund-raising techniques are to identify the organization and the reason for the call up front; make a direct request for a specific contribution; and alter the request, if necessary, to try to get a positive response.

Key Terms

closing	personal selling
cue	preselling
customer profiles	point-of-sale market research
direct mail	proactive telemarketing
market research	reactive telemarketing
market segmentation	telemarketing agency
market survey	telemarketing service bureau
objections	telephone survey

Chapter Review

Write your answers to the questions that follow and be prepared to discuss them in class.

1. Explain the difference between proactive and reactive telemarketing. List some examples of each from your personal experience.

2. You are selling membership in a computer game club. Each month members are sent a brochure of new computer games which they can order through direct mail or by calling your 800 number. You have before you a target list of customers that recently purchased home computers. Make a list of questions that you could ask to identify the customers' need for your product.

3. You are one of the telemarketers conducting the survey of channel 57 viewers shown on pages 118-119. You have a list of 200 people to call. Out of ten calls placed so far, six people have responded that they would be happy to answer your questions, but they do not have cable TV in their area. What steps can you take to avoid continuing to waste time calling people who cannot respond to the questionnaire?

4. **You are helping your supervisor develop a training session for a group of volunteers who are going to staff a telemarketing campaign to raise funds for a community youth center. Your supervisor has written a list of possible objections that the telemarketers will need to respond to. She has asked you to compile a list of statements for each objection.**

Objection: I don't have time to talk to you right now.

Response: _____

Objection: I contribute to the United Way on my job.

Response: _____

Objection: I can't afford to contribute anything.

Response: _____

Objection: I'm moving out of this area in a couple of weeks.

Response: _____

5. **The *Westside Reporter*, a local newspaper, wanted to increase its circulation. Its telemarketing staff was given a survey questionnaire and told to interview nonsubscribers about their reading habits. To their surprise, each potential customer who participated in the survey received in the mail a "free" copy of the newspaper, along with an "automatic" subscription. They must return a "cancel my subscription card" within ten days or they will be billed for a year's subscription. Explain how this action violates specific articles of the Guidelines for Telephone Marketing Practices.**

_____

_____

_____

_____

_____

| **Audio Dialogue 7-2** | Read the background information below. Then turn on your audiocassette player and listen to Audio Dialogue 7-2. Turn off the player when the end of the dialogue is announced. (Do not rewind the cassette.) Then answer the questions below. |

Background: Mary Ann Vacarro is conducting a survey for a utilities company. The company is tracking changes in the usage of electric power over a two-year period.

| **Audio Analysis 7-2** | You are Mary Ann's supervisor and you were listening in on this call. Write an evaluation in list or paragraph form for Mary Ann, stating her strengths and weaknesses in conducting the interview. Point out any specific problems that occurred in the interview and indicate how she might have avoided them. |

_____

_____

_____

_____

_____

_____

_____

_____

_____

_____

_____

| **Audio Dialogue 7-3** | Read the background information below. Then turn on your audiocassette player and listen to Audio Dialogue 7-3. Turn off the player when the end of the dialogue is announced. (Do not rewind the cassette.) Then answer the questions on the following page. |

Background: Craig Roberts works for the Wildlife Conservation Society as a telemarketing sales representative. The Society's goal is to raise funds by increasing the Society's membership in the metropolitan area of a major city.

List the strengths and weaknesses of Craig's fund-raising solicitation.

1. Strengths:

_____

_____

_____

_____

2. Weaknesses:

_____

_____

_____

_____

3. As Craig's supervisor, write a script to help him improve his presentation of the identity of the organization and the purpose of the call.

Identify the organization:

_____

_____

_____

_____

_____

_____

Identify the purpose of the call:

_____

_____

_____

_____

CUSTOMER SERVICE

On the Job: Dealing with Customers

Ernest Moreno is the head of administrative services for Doctors Hospital in Denver, Colorado. He is responsible for ensuring that the nonmedical aspects of the hospital run smoothly. He oversees policies, procedures, and employees.

Moreno: Doctors Hospital. Ernest Moreno speaking.

Banks: Is this the head of administrative services?

Moreno: Yes, it is.

Banks: My name is Diana Banks. I had a test at your hospital on July 8. I received a bill for $480 and paid it on August 3. Three months later I received a bill for a test I did not have. The amount was $520. I wrote a letter explaining that I did not have the test I was billed for. A month later I received a second bill for the same test I did not have.

Moreno: Yes?

Banks: I called and explained what happened to someone in your billing department. That person called up my account on the computer and told me that the charge would be deleted. A month later I got yet another bill. I called again, and the same thing happened. And it happened still once again. Now I got a note saying that if I don't pay the bill, my account will be turned over to a collection agency, and my credit rating is at risk. What do I have to do to get this to stop?

Moreno: I'm terribly sorry that you are having so much trouble.

Banks: Everyone I've talked to has been sorry. But no one seems to be able to put an end to the situation.

Moreno: I think that your patient number must have been mistakenly assigned to another patient.

Banks: I don't care about how this happened. I just want it to stop.

Moreno: I assure you, Ms. Banks, that the error will be corrected.

Banks: I've heard that before.

Moreno: What if I send you a letter assuring you that you are not responsible for the amount that is owed.

Banks: So I will have something in writing that says that I don't owe this money?

Moreno: Yes. Would that be okay?

Banks: Yes. I think it would make me feel more comfortable about the whole situation if I had something in writing.

Moreno: Good. Now, I am going to switch you to Elaine Goldin. She is the head of our billing department. She'll take all the necessary information from you.

Banks: I don't trust anybody in your billing department.

Moreno: I assure you, Ms. Banks, that Ms. Goldin will be able to help you. And I promise that I will personally check to make sure that the problem is taken care of. I will get your address from Ms. Goldin and send you the letter immediately.

Banks: Well, as long as you're going to check on it, I guess that will be all right.

Moreno: I'm very sorry about the whole situation. Now, please hold on while I switch you to Ms. Goldin.

Banks: OK. Thanks.

Ernest Moreno handled the problem with Ms. Banks skillfully. He apologized for the mistake and figured out what would make Ms. Banks feel better about the situation—the letter and his assurance that he will make sure that the problem has been corrected. Mr. Moreno learned a lesson from this phone call. The administrative employees in the hospital needed to improve their customer service skills.

Objectives

After completing this chapter, you should be able to:

- Recognize the importance of learning about your company, your department, the product or service being sold, and your equipment.

- Enumerate and explain the most common functions of a customer service department, including providing information, taking orders, handling customer accounts, handling complaints, and telemarketing.

- Identify the job qualifications for a customer service representative.

- Distinguish between the procedural training and on-the-job training that customer service representatives receive.

- Identify how customer service departments may be organized.

- Understand how customer service representatives must deal with stress.

- Identify the do's and don'ts for dealing with customers and clients.

◼ General Procedures

Because of difficult economic conditions and a highly competitive business environment, many companies have placed special emphasis on offering customers the best possible service. Managers believe that the service they offer can give them an edge over the competition. The goal of customer service is to create and maintain satisfied, loyal customers with a positive view of the company and its products.

Any worker who comes in contact with the public is involved in customer service. This aspect of a worker's job may be limited to an occasional incoming call, or it may be a full-time career in a customer service department. Regardless of the job you hold, you can contribute to your company's positive image with customers by following some general procedures and guidelines.

LEARN ABOUT YOUR COMPANY

Whether you work for a large or small company, it is advisable to learn as much as you can about your company. In a small company, find out who is responsible for what. In a large company, learn about the different divisions and departments. Get a general idea of the products handled by different divisions. With this information, you will be able to forward calls to the appropriate individual or department without bouncing the customer from one person to the next.

Many companies have phone books and/or organization charts that indicate who is responsible for various goods and services. In addition, larger companies usually offer some form of orientation for new employees. These orientation sessions will most likely introduce you to the different parts of the company and the goods or services offered.

LEARN ABOUT YOUR DEPARTMENT

Experienced employees know about their own departments simply from being on the job. New employees will not necessarily know about the department they have joined. They may only know about the particular job they were hired to perform.

If you find yourself in a situation where you are not given information about your department, you may ask your manager or a coworker to fill you in. If, as a new employee, you find a customer calling with a question you cannot answer, do not attempt to "wing it." Explain to the customer that you are new on the job and that you will transfer him or her to someone who can help. You can also consider listening to the customer's concerns and then explain that you will get the information necessary and get back to the customer. Never respond unless you are sure of your answer.

LEARN ABOUT THE PRODUCT OR SERVICE

If the department in which you work deals in products, you may be able to learn about the product line by reviewing the catalog or sales brochures and other marketing information. If your department deals in a service, again, you may be able to refer to printed sales or marketing information to learn about the services provided.

Figure 8-1

Become familiar with the product or service your company sells before speaking with potential customers.

Photo by Alan Brown/Photonics.

LEARN ABOUT YOUR EQUIPMENT

The two key pieces of office equipment essential in providing good service to customers are the telephone and the computer. You should understand the telephone system, know what kinds of special features your telephone has, and learn how to use them. Of particular importance are the procedures for putting someone on hold and for tranferrring a call. In both cases, you do not want to make a mistake and disconnect a customer. Refer to Chapter 4 for guidelines on putting callers on hold and transferring calls.

Many customer files are on computer. Computers are also used in order departments. It is critical that you understand how to use the computer and software so that you can accurately update and/or change customer information and take orders.

Figure 8-2

This illustration shows specially designed software for the order process that is used by customer service representatives.

MARQUETTE'S ORDER ENTRY

CUSTOMER NO._____ ORDER NO._____ ORDER

DATE_____

ORDER TYPE_____ ORDER STATUS_____

DISCOUNT_____

SHIP TO: _____   BILL TO: _____

_____   _____

_____   _____

P.O. NO. _____ SHIP VIA _____ TEL. NO. _____

SHPG.CHG. _____ TOTAL SALE_____

ITEM NBR QTY SHP PRICE EXTENDED DESCRIPTION

■ Customer Service Departments

Customer service departments can vary greatly in size and in function. The most common functions of customer service departments are:

- **Providing information:** For example, many computer software companies have 24-hour, 800-number helplines for software users.

- **Taking orders:** Many mail-order companies have departments that exclusively take orders over the phone.

- **Handling customer accounts:** This may include questions or problems about billing, shipping, damaged merchandise, and the like.

- **Handling complaints:** This may include some issues covered in customer accounts as well as different kinds of complaints. For example, cable television companies may have special departments that deal only with TV reception problems; TV networks may have departments that handle complaints from viewers.

- **Telemarketing:** As discussed in Chapter 7, this involves selling over the phone.

As more and more companies use the telephone for sales, taking orders, and providing customers with information, more and more jobs will be created. In addition to seeking qualified job candidates, customer service departments provide training for the people they hire.

411

In an effort to provide customers with the best and most accessible service possible, companies have instituted a variety of telephone services that are designed to satisfy customers. Customer service and the telephone are closely linked as the desire for one has led to numerous business opportunities for the other.

As of 1994, more than 500,000 businesses and government agencies have more than 1.3 million 800 numbers. Many of these provide 24-hour service.

In further efforts to satisfy customer demands for extended service hours, many companies utilize telephone and computer systems software such as voice response units (VRU), voice mail, and electronic order systems. These services enable customers to access general or account information, leave messages, or place orders 24 hours a day without having a live customer service representative on the premises.

JOB QUALIFICATIONS

Since customer service departments vary in function, some specific **job qualifications** will differ from one place to the next. However, as a rule, managers of customer service departments are looking for people with the following qualifications:

- **Previous experience (about a year) in customer service.** This may include phone work, personal selling, representing products, or credit or collection phone work.

- **Ability to express themselves.** Managers want to hire people who are articulate and who have good vocabularies. It is acceptable for job candidates to have accents as long as they are able to be understood and can understand others. The two most important qualities are tone of voice and the ability to sound interested and helpful. Some managers can often tell from the phone call they receive to set up the job interview whether a candidate will be appropriate for the job.

- **Maturity.** This is not an issue of age but one of attitude. Good customer service representatives must be able to maintain their composure under pressure. They must also be able to understand and accept that different people react in many, often extreme, ways when they are upset.

Job candidates who express themselves well and appear mature may be hired even without previous experience.

TRAINING

Newly hired customer service representatives will receive some training regardless of whether they have previous experience as customer service representatives. Training programs may vary in length—some may take only a few weeks; others may last as long as several months.

Training for customer service workers is usually divided into two parts: procedural training and on-the-job training.

Procedural Training

Procedural training often covers three different elements:

1. Learning about the company and the products or services being offered.

2. Learning about the policies that specifically apply to customer issues or problems—what you may or may not do in certain situations. For example, the company may have guidelines about how much you can do to satisfy a customer if the customer is upset as a result of a mistake made by your company. This would differ from how much you can do to satisfy a customer if your company is not responsible for the problem.

   Policies may also include what specific things you should never say.

3. Learning about the equipment you will be using. This includes the telephone system and the computer system and software.

In order to keep their hands free to work computers or write, customer service reps wear headsets. **Headsets** may fit over the head or under the chin. They are designed so that the earpieces are covered with a soft material that is comfortable to wear.

On-the-Job Training

After newly hired representatives receive their procedural training, they continue their **on-the-job training** by taking calls. The calls are monitored by their supervisors, who may participate in the call to keep the representative on track. Special or difficult problems are discussed so that the rep can be prepared for similar situations in the future.

Don Wyler works in the order department of Lawrence's, a retail clothing chain with stores throughout the southwest. Lawrence's has expanded its business by distributing a mail-order catalog and serves customers in all parts of the country. Don was hired to process the orders received by mail. Recently, Lawrence's instituted an 800 number for phone orders. Don is familiar with the company and its product line. He has also been trained to use the phone and computer systems. He has not received much training in dealing with customers and has not had any on-the-job training. He was instructed to be polite to customers and to try to keep the calls brief since he has a lot of other work to do. Soon after the 800 number is announced to customers, he receives the following call from Ursella Harper:

Figure 8-3

Headsets free representatives to use their hands.

Don: Lawrence's. How may I help you?
Ursella: I'd like to place an order, please.
Don: Have you ever placed an order with us before?
Ursella: Yes, by mail.
Don: Then you would have a customer account number with us.
Ursella: I do? How do I know what it is?
Don: It's on the mailing label of your catalog, right above and to the right of your name.
Ursella: Oh, here it is. It's twelve oh nine seven four three two.
Don: Twelve oh nine seven four three two.
Ursella: Right.
Don: You're Ursella Harper. 1171 Markhan Court, Charlottesville, Virginia 22912.
Ursella: That's right.
Don: Now, what is the style number of the first item you would like to order?
Ursella: Wait, let me find it. Here it is. It's M one twenty-nine oh eight.
Don: M one twenty-nine oh eight.
Ursella: Uh huh.
Don: Description?
Ursella: They're slacks.
Don: There's an item description, like an item name, in boldface type in the catalog.
Ursella: Oh, wait. Here. Misses gabardine pants.
Don: Color?
Ursella: Navy.
Don: Size?
Ursella: Ten.

Don: How many pairs do you want?

Ursella: One pair.

Don: Do you want to order anything else?

Ursella: Yes. A blouse.

Don: Style number?

Ursella: One second. Let me find the page.

Don: The next time you order something from us, I'd like to suggest that you fill out the mail order form even if you're ordering by phone. This way you have all the information you need right in front of you.

Ursella: Okay. I turned down the corner of the page. Here, the style number is M three forty-two one six.

Don: M three forty-two one six. Ma'am, we're out of stock on that item. It will be six to eight weeks before we can fill that order.

Ursella: Well, I don't want to wait that long. Oh, dear. That was a blouse I was ordering to go with the slacks. If you don't have the blouse, then I don't want the slacks either.

Don: You want me to cancel the order for the slacks?

Ursella: Yes. But wait. I saw another outfit that I liked but I wasn't planning to buy both. Since I'm not getting the first one, let me see if I can find the second one.

Don: Maybe it would be better if you call back once you find what you're looking for.

Ursella: Can't you hold on a minute?

Don: I think it would be better if you called back.

Ursella: Don't count on it. (She hangs up.)

1. Do you think it was appropriate for Don to suggest that Ursella fill out the order form the next time she places a phone order? Why or why not?

_____

_____

_____

2. Was it acceptable for Don to suggest that Ursella call back? Was Ursella justified in becoming angry? Explain.

_____

_____

_____

3. How might training have helped Don handle this call so that the result would not have been an angry customer?

_____

_____

_____

Figure 8-4

Customer service

department.

Photo by Alan Brown/Photonics.

ORGANIZATION OF DEPARTMENTS

Customer service departments are organized in different ways. Some may consist of small work groups in which each group reports to a different supervisor. This kind of departmental setup fosters close supervision and considerable interaction between the reps and the supervisors.

Other departments are set up in large groups with few supervisors. Because the supervisors are responsible for large numbers of reps, it is not possible for them to oversee their departments as closely as supervisors of small groups. Often in large groups, reps may be assigned to higher levels, such as senior rep. This position is not a full supervisory position but does help with some coaching responsibilities.

The organization of customer service departments may also differ in the responsibilities of the workers. Some departments are set up to handle phone calls exclusively. Others are organized so that the workers do a variety of customer-oriented tasks in addition to phone work. This may include keeping customer accounts and handling incoming mail.

DEALING WITH STRESS

Customer service telephone work can be highly stressful, especially for those representatives who work in complaint departments or in departments that have a high, steady volume of calls. Management is aware of the high stress levels, which are demonstrated through high turnover and absentee rates.

In order to help workers cope with the **stress,** managers may implement a number of measures. For example, breaks at regular intervals can alleviate some of the pressure. Some companies have workers do exercises for brief periods. This is very helpful in eliminating stress and prevents discomfort when workers have to sit for long periods of time.

Many companies have regularly scheduled group meetings where workers are encouraged to discuss the problems they have been dealing with. Not only does this help to eliminate stress, but sharing their experiences provides other workers with valuable information that may help them deal with similar situations.

Figure 8-5

Customer service

representatives and

managers discuss

problems they have

had with cus-

tomers.

Photo by Alan Brown/Photonics.

Some phone systems enable a customer service worker to signal for a manager. The signal may be a light going on, which tells the supervisor that assistance is needed. The supervisor can help the rep cope with a difficult situation. This help signal is also useful in providing assistance or information to a rep without the rep having to put the caller on hold.

Dealing with Customers

Because customer service work encompasses so many different areas, the term "customer" should be regarded loosely. Federal, state, and local governments and nonprofit organizations do not technically have customers. However, it is just as important for them to enlist the goodwill of the public as it is for private businesses to seek the goodwill of its customers or potential customers.

DO'S AND DON'TS

Regardless of the kind of job you have or the kind of organization you work for, your job will be to present a positive, helpful impression to the people you deal with over the phone. Following are some guidelines that will help you in your dealings with customers.

Do's

Do apologize to customers for the problems they are having. This applies even if the problem is not your fault or the fault of your company. "I'm sorry to hear that you lost the statement we sent you."

Do focus on resolving the problem rather than on the problem itself. "I'll put a duplicate statement in the mail to you today."

Do accept responsibility if a problem is the fault of something that your company did. "I'm terribly sorry that the shipment was damaged in transit."

Do take the initiative (within reason) to resolve the problem, especially if your company is at fault. "We will send you a duplicate shipment using an overnight delivery service, so you will have it tomorrow. And we will not charge you for shipping and handling."

Do negotiate a resolution if the problem was not your company's fault. "I'm sorry to hear that your receiving department was flooded and that your shipment was damaged. We can arrange to send you a dupicate shipment overnight, but the delivery charges will be higher than for standard delivery. Will that be OK?"

Don'ts

Don't be defensive if your company is at fault. Customers are not interested in why something happened. They just want their problems resolved.

Don't take anything that customers say personally. They are angry at a problem or situation, not at you. This can be very difficult to achieve. One of the reasons that customer service work is so stressful is that workers take anger personally.

Don't tell customers that your company or department policy does not allow you to do something. Hearing this just makes people angrier than they already are. Even if your company has a policy that will prevent you from doing something, talk around it or suggest an alternative to what the customer is asking for.

Don't suggest that customers are lying or that they don't know what they are talking about. It's better to suggest that something is a misunderstanding.

Don't assume that all problems can be resolved or that all customers will be satisfied. It is simply not possible to fix everything and make everyone happy.

Don't allow yourself to be drawn into an angry interchange. It's all right to become angry so long as you behave appropriately and say the correct things in a normal tone of voice.

Read the background information below. Then turn on your audiocassette player and listen to Audio Dialogue 8-1 on. Turn off the player when the end of the dialogue is announced. (Do not rewind the cassette.) Then answer the questions on the following page.

> **Audio Dialogue 8-1**

Background: Wendy Royce has worked for Milford Electronics Repair Service for almost 15 years. Milford is a medium-sized repair company that fixes TVs, stereo equipment, CD players, VCRs, radios, and other electronic appliances. Milford has arrangements with appliance dealers in the area to handle the service contracts that customers may elect to buy when they buy a new piece of equipment.

The conditions of service contracts vary, but the contracts generally state that the repair service will provide in-home repair or pickup and return of serviced equipment. Customers may get a contract for one or two years. The contracts are renewable. One of Wendy's jobs is to notify customers that their contracts are about to expire and find out if the customer wants to renew. She has developed excellent selling skills in convincing customers of the benefits of renewing their service contracts. Wendy also handles some of the accounts receivable and payable, and she orders office supplies and answers the phone. Most of the time incoming calls are fairly routine—making appointments for customers to have equipment picked up for repair or returned after the work has been completed.

Wendy never received any special training in customer service. She has learned to deal with customers over the course of time.

<table>
<tr><td>

Audio Analysis 8-1

</td><td>

1. Do you think that Wendy offered more than she should have by offering to transfer the contract? Explain your answer.

_____

_____

_____

2. If Wendy had not offered to transfer the contract, what else, if anything, might she have suggested?

_____

_____

3. If Wendy had not offered to transfer the contract, do you think Doris would have been interested in recommending Milford to her friend? Why or why not?

_____

_____

_____

</td></tr>
</table>

HANDLING PROBLEM CALLS

During the course of your career, you are likely to receive calls from people who are angry, frustrated, confused, demanding, abusive, unreasonable, and just plain unpleasant. You will need to draw on all your communications and human relations skills to deal with such callers. The do's and don'ts noted previously, plus the communications skills discussed throughout this book, should help you maneuver your way through all kinds of problems.

Remember to focus on the solution, not the problem.

■ Chapter Summary

- Any worker who comes in contact with customers or the public is, in a sense, involved in customer service.

- Workers should learn as much as they can about their company, their department, the goods or services offered by the company, and their telephone equipment so that they will be prepared to deal with customers effectively.

- The most common functions of customer service departments are to provide information, take orders, handle customer accounts, handle complaints, and sell goods or services (telemarketing).

- Three job qualifications for customer service representatives are experience (about one year), the ability to express oneself well, and maturity.

- Customer service representatives receive two kinds of training—procedural and on-the-job. Procedural training covers such things as learning about the company, learning about the goods or services offered, learning about the company or department policies concerning dealing with customers, and learning about the telephone equipment. On-the-job training has the representative working with customers while being advised and monitored by a supervisor.

- Customer service departments are organized in different ways: One common departmental organization is to have workers in small groups with close supervision; another is to have large groups with fewer supervisors.

- In order to help customer service representatives cope with stress, managers allow workers breaks throughout the day, organize exercise periods, and conduct discussion groups in which workers can discuss their problems.

- In dealing with customers, customer service representatives should apologize; focus on solving a problem, not the problem itself; accept responsibility when the company is at fault; take the initiative in resolving problems; and negotiate a resolution.

- In dealing with customers, customer service representatives should not become defensive, take things personally, tell customers that they can or cannot do something because of company policy, suggest that customers are lying, assume that all problems can be resolved, or get into an argument.

■ Key Terms

headsets
job qualifications
on-the-job training
procedural training
stress

Chapter Review

Write your answers to the questions that follow and be prepared to discuss them in class.

1. **Name and describe briefly the two different kinds of training customer service representatives receive.**

_____

_____

_____

_____

_____

2. **List two do's and two don'ts in customer service.**

_____

_____

_____

_____

_____

_____

3. **It is suggested that you apologize to a customer for a problem even if you or your company is not responsible for the problem. Do you agree with this approach? Explain why or why not.**

_____

_____

_____

_____

_____

4. **List three different functions of customer service departments and briefly describe each. Can you think of any not mentioned in this chapter? If so, list and describe these as well.**

_____

5. Customer service jobs can be very stressful. They can also be interesting and challenging. Would you consider a job as a customer service representative? Explain why or why not.

Read the background information below. Then turn on your audiocassette player and listen to Audio Dialogue 8-2. Turn off the player when the end of the dialogue is announced. (Do not rewind the cassette.) Then answer the questions below.

Audio Dialogue 8-2

Background: Marvin Jones has been a postal clerk for five years at the Hawthorne Station, one of the many local branches in Chicago. None of the workers at the station is specifically assigned to answer the phone. The telephone is not a big part of any postal clerk's job, since the phone does not ring all that often. Although postal workers are instructed to be polite and helpful to the public, no special training or guidelines are provided for phone work.

It is the second week in December, and the post office is in the midst of the Christmas season overload of mail. Marvin and many of the other workers are putting in long hours of overtime.

I. Do you think that there is a resolution to this problem? Explain why or why not.

Audio Analysis 8-2

2. What in the conversation did Marvin do right? What did he do wrong? Explain why you think he was right or wrong.

_____

_____

_____

_____

_____

3. Regardless of whether you think there is a resolution to the problem, what could Marvin have said so that the conversation did not end in such a negative way?

_____

_____

_____

_____

_____

4. Should Marvin have lied and said that he would look for the invitation even though he knew he wouldn't actually do it?

_____

_____

_____

_____

_____

5. Should Marvin have offered to look for the invitation? Explain why you think he should or should not.

_____

_____

_____

_____

_____

APPENDIX A

AREA CODES FOR MAJOR CITIES IN THE UNITED STATES AND TERRITORIES

State	City	Code
Alabama	All locations	205
Alaska	All locations	907
Arizona	All locations	602
Arkansas	All locations	501
California	Beverly Hills	310
	Burbank (L.A. County)	818
	East Los Angeles	213
	Oakland	510
	Palm Springs	619
	Pasadena	818
	Sacramento	916
	San Francisco	415
	Santa Barbara	805
Colorado	Aspen	303
	Colorado Springs	719
	Denver	303
	Ft. Collins	970
Connecticut	All locations	203
Delaware	All locations	302
District of Columbia	Washington, D.C.	202
Florida	Boca Raton	407
	Daytona Beach	904
	Fort Lauderdale	305
	Miami	305
	Orlando	407

State	City	Code
Florida *continued*	Tallahassee	904
Georgia	Athens	706
	Atlanta	404
	Columbus	706
	Savannah	912
Hawaii	All locations	808
Idaho	All locations	208
Illinois	Bloomington	309
	Champaigne-Urbana	217
	Chicago	312
	Peoria	309
Indiana	Gary	219
	Indianapolis	317
	South Bend	219
	Terre Haute	812
Iowa	Ames	515
	Cedar Rapids	319
	Des Moines	515
	Iowa City	319
	Sioux City	712
Kansas	Kansas City	913
	Wichita	316
Kentucky	Bowling Green	502
	Lexington	606
	Louisville	502
Louisiana	Baton Rouge	504
	New Orleans	504
	Shreveport	318
Maine	All locations	207
Maryland	Annapolis	410
	Baltimore	410
Massachusetts	Amherst	413
	Boston	617
Michigan	Detroit	313
	Grand Rapids	616
	Lansing	517
	Kalamazoo	616
Minnesota	Duluth	218
	Minneapolis	612
	St. Paul	612
Missisippi	All locations	601
Missouri	Kansas City	816
	St. Louis	314
Montana	All locations	406
Nebraska	Lincoln	402

State	City	Code
	Omaha	402
Nevada	All locations	702
New Hampshire	All locations	603
New Jersey	Atlantic City	609
	Newark	201
	Trenton	609
New York	Albany	518
	Brooklyn	718
	Buffalo	716
	Manhattan	212
	Rochester	716
North Carolina	Charlotte	704
	Raleigh	919
North Dakota	All locations	701
Ohio	Cincinnati	513
	Cleveland	216
	Columbus	614
	Dayton	513
Oklahoma	Oklahoma City	405
	Tulsa	918
Oregon	All locations	503
Pennsylvania	Philadelphia	215
	Pittsburgh	412
Puerto Rico	All locations	809
Rhode Island	All locations	401
South Carolina	All locations	803
South Dakota	All locations	605
Tennessee	Memphis	901
	Nashville	615
Texas	Austin	512
	Dallas	214
	Fort Worth	817
	Houston	713
Utah	All locations	801
Vermont	All locations	802
Virgin Islands	All locations	809
Virginia	Arlington	703
	Norfolk	804
	Richmond	804
Washington	Seattle	206
	Spokane	509
	Tacoma	206
West Virginia	All locations	304
Wiscon	Green Bay	414
	Madison	609
Wyoming	All locations	308

APPENDIX B

INTERNATIONAL CALLING CODES FOR COUNTRIES AND MAJOR CITIES

Country	Code	City	Code
Algeria	213		None required
Argentina	54	Buenos Aires	1
Aruba	297	Aruba	8
Australia	61	Melbourne	3
		Sydney	2
Austria	43	Vienna	1
Belgium	32	Brussels	2
Belize	501		None required
Bolivia	591	Santa Cruz	33
Brazil	55	Brasilia	61
		Rio De Janeiro	21
Chile	56	Santiago	2
Colombia	57	Bogota	1
Costa Rica	506		None required
Cyprus	357		None required
Denmark	45	Copenhagen	1 or 2
Ecuador	593	Quito	2
Egypt	20	Alexandria	3
		Port Said	66

Country	Code	City	Code
El Salvador	503		None required
Finland	358	Helsinki	0
France	33	Nice	93
		Paris	13, 14, or 16
Germany	49	Berlin	30
Greece	30	Athens	1
Guam	671		None required
Guatemala	502	Guatemala City	2
		Antigua	9
Guyana	592	Georgetown	2
Haiti	509	Port au Prince	1
Honduras	504		None required
Hong Kong	852		None required
Hungary	36	Budapest	1
India	91	Bombay	22
		New Delhi	11
Indonesia	62	Jakarta	21
Iran	98	Teheran	21
Iraq	964	Baghdad	1
Ireland	353	Dublin	1
Israel	972	Jerusalem	2
		Tel Aviv	3
Italy	39	Florence	55
		Rome	6
		Venice	41
Ivory Coast	225		None required
Japan	81	Tokyo	3
		Yokohama	45
Jordan	962	Amman	6
Kenya	254		None required
Korea (South)	82	Seoul	2
Kuwait	965		None required

Country	Code	City	Code
Libya	218	Tripoli	21
Malaysia	60	Kuala Lumpur	3
Mexico	52	Mexico City	5
		Tijuana	66
Monaco	33	All	93
Morocco	212	Agadir	8
Netherlands	31	Amsterdam	20
		The Hague	70
New Zealand	64	Auckland	9
Nicaragua	505	Managua	2
Nigeria	234	Lagos	1
Norway	47	Oslo	2
Pakistan	92	Islamabad	51
Panama	507		None required
Paraguay	595	Asuncion	21
Peru	51	Lima	14
Philippines	63	Manila	2
Poland	48	Warsaw	22
Portugal	351	Lisbon	1
Saudi Arabia	966	Riyadh	1
Singapore	65		None required
South Africa	27	Cape Town	21
Spain	34	Barcelona	3
		Madrid	1
		Seville	54
Sweden	46	Stockholm	8
Switzerland	41	Geneva	22
		Zurich	1
Thailand	66	Bangkok	2
Turkey	90	Istanbul	1

Country	Code	City	Code
United Kingdom	44	Glasgow	41
		London	71 or 81
Uruguay	598	Montevideo	2
Venezuela	58	Caracas	2

APPENDIX C

THE 24-HOUR CLOCK

A.M.

24-Hour Clock	12-Hour Clock
0100	1:00 a.m.
0200	2:00 a.m.
0300	3:00 a.m.
0400	4:00 a.m.
0500	5:00 a.m.
0600	6:00 a.m.
0700	7:00 a.m.
0800	8:00 a.m.
0900	9:00 a.m.
1000	10:00 a.m.
1100	11:00 a.m.
1200	12:00 noon

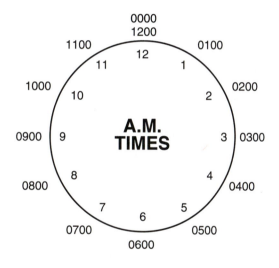

P.M.

24-Hour Clock	12-Hour Clock
1300	1:00 p.m.
1400	2:00 p.m.
1500	3:00 p.m.
1600	4:00 p.m.
1700	5:00 p.m.
1800	6:00 p.m.
1900	7:00 p.m.
2000	8:00 p.m.
2100	9:00 p.m.
2200	10:00 p.m.
2300	11:00 p.m.
2400	12:00 midnight

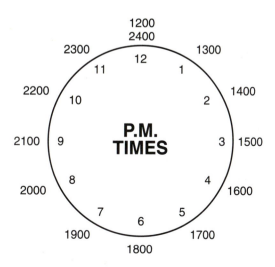

Credit: *Destination: North America*
by Dawne M. Flammger, Delmar Publishers, New York, 1993.

INDEX

A

Accents, 46-47
Administrative phone procedures, 74-77
Airphones, 25
Air travel, 82-83
Answering for the manager, 74
Appointments, scheduling, 80-82
Area codes
    international, 151-154
    U.S. cities, 147-149
Arrangements, making over the phone, 80-84
Attention, 48
Attitude, 9, 47
Audible distractions, 47
Automated attendant, 18-19
Automatic callback, 22

B

Beepers, 26
Being put on the spot, 58-59
Benefits, 111-112
Blue pages, 78
Business customs, 97-98
Business hours, international, 97

C

Call director, 20
Caller ID, 23
Call forwarding, 22
Call record system, 23
Calls
    making, 60-65
    planning, 65-66
    receiving, 55-60
Call transfer, 22
Call waiting, 22

Cellular phones, 25-26
Centralized communications systems, 18-19
Charge number, 82
Closing (sale), 112
Collect calls, 63
Communication
    avoiding distractions, 41-42
    effective, 39-41
    feedback in, 40-41
    process of, 39
    speaking skills, 42-47
Communications
    external, 5-6
    internal, 5
Communications process, 4
Communications skills
    basic skills, 8-9
    quality approach to, 7-8
    speaking, 42-47
    telephone persona, 9-10
Communications systems, 18
    centralized, 18-19
    decentralized, 19-21
Competence, 10
Conference attendant, 30
Conferencing, 22
Confidentiality, 67
Credit card calls, 63
Creditor calls, 59-60
Cue, 112
Cultural differences, 99-100
Customer profiles, 110
Customer service, 131-132
    customer service departments, 135-140
    dealing with customers, 140-142
    general procedures, 133-134

D

Decentralized communications systems, 19-21
Dedicated lines, 26
Direct calls, 62
Direct dial, 19, 93
Direct mail, 109
Direct Marketing Association, Inc., 122
  Mail Preference Service name-removal list, 123-124
Directories, 77-79
Distractions, 41-42

E

English language, 100
Enunciation, 43
Exchange, 19
Extension number, 19-20
External communications, 5-6

F

Facsimile (fax) machines, 26-27, 64-65
Facsimile transmission, 26-28
Fax attendant, 27
Fax response, 28
Feedback, 40-41, 48
Fund-raising, 111
  steps in, 120-121
  techniques for, 120

G

Global village, 97
Grammar, 43-44

H

Headsets, 136
Highways, 3
Hold button, 22
Hotel reservations, 83-84

I

Image, 10
Individual pickup, 20
Information, locating, 79-80
Information Age, 3
Information Superhighway, 3
Information warehouses, 3
Infotainment, 3
Interactive Age, 3
Interactive technology, 3
Intercom, 22
Intercultural communications
  cultural differences, 99-100
  international business procedures, 97-98

language barriers, 100-101
learning about other cultures, 101
Interfaces, 3
Internal communications, 5
International business procedures, 97-98
International calling procedures, 92
International dateline, 95
International telephone communications
  area codes list, 151-154
  crossing time zones, 94-96
  locating information, 93
  placing international calls, 93
  24-hour clock, 96, 155
  using translation services, 94
Interoffice calls, 61

J

Job qualifications, 135

L

Language barriers, 100-101
Last number redial, 22
Leaving messages, 66
Listening skills, 9, 48
Local calls, 61
Local carriers, 30
Locating information, 79-80
Locating people, 78-79
Long-distance calls, 61-63
Long-distance carriers, 30

M

Making calls, 60-65
Market research, 111
  point-of-sale, 116-117
  telephone surveys, 117-120
Market segmentation, 110
Market survey, 111
Meetings, scheduling, 80-82
Message alert, 22
Messages, 66, 75
Mobile telephone equipment, 25-26
Modulation, 42-43
Multilingual display, 23

N

National expressions, 45-46
Networks, 2
New York Times, 101

O

Objections, 112
On-line computer information services, 80
On-the-job training, 136
Operator-assisted calls, 93

Orders, placing, 84
Organization, 9
Outgoing calls, 60-63
Overcoming objections, 112

P

Pace, 42
Pagers, 26
People, locating, 78-79
Personal selling, 109
Person-to-person calls, 62
Phone coverage, 56-57
Placing orders, 84
Planning calls, 65-66
Point-of-sale market research, 116-117
Preselling, 112
Proactive telemarketing, 109
Problem calls, 60, 142
Problem-solving, 9
Procedural training, 136
Pronunciation, 43
Putting callers on hold, 57

R

Reactive telemarketing, 109-110
Receiving calls, 55-60
Records, telephone, 76-77
Regional expressions, 44
Rejection, handling, 112
Research, telephone, 77-80
Reservations, making, 82-84
Ring designation, 22
Rotary telephone, 19

S

Sale closing, 112
Sales, 111
Scheduling meetings/appointments, 80-82
Screening calls, 21, 74-75
Seven-step selling process, 112-115
Speakerphones, 23
Speaking skills, 9, 42-47
Special situations, 75-76
Speed (abbreviated) dialing, 22
Standard telephone equipment/features,
    22-23
Stress, 139-140
Successful Telemarketing (Stone &
    Wyman), 112

T

Taking the initiative, 75
Technology, 97
Telecommunications defined, 2
    technology, 26-29
Teleconferencing, 29-30
    handling, 84-85

Teleconferencing bridges, 30
Telemarketing
    communication skills for, 110-111
    defined, 109
    field of, 121-124
    fund-raising by, 120-121
    market research by, 116-120
    selling by, 111-115
    types of, 109-110
    uses of, 111
Telemarketing agencies, 121
Telemarketing service bureaus, 121
Telephone
    answering, 55-56
    as communications tool, 4-6
    equipment, 22-26
    service providers, 30
Telephone communication skills
    avoiding distractions, 41-42
    effective communication, 39-41
    listening skills, 48
    speaking skills, 42-47
Telephone directories, 77-79
Telephone log, 76-77
Telephone message forms, 57
Telephone persona, 9-10
Telephone research, 77-80
Telephone surveys, 117-120
Telephone tag, 21
Tie-lines, 61
Time management, 9
Time zones, 61-62
    crossing, 94-96
Tone of voice, 9, 43
Total Quality Management (TQM), 7
Touch-Tone telephone, 19
Trade associations, 93
Training, 136
Transferring calls, 58
Translation services, 94
24-hour clock, 96, 155

U

Unwanted callers, 59-60

V

Vendor calls, 59
Verbal distractions, 47
Videophones, 23-24
Vocabulary, 44
Voice information systems, 29
Voice mail, 8, 21
    using, 56
Voice messaging systems, 28-29
Voice processing, 28-29

W

Writing, 9